Here's How

Have a Winning Job Interview

DEBORAH P. BLOCH, PH.D.

NTC LEARNINGWORKS
NTC/Contemporary Publishing Company

Library of Congress Cataloging-in-Publication Data
is available from the United States Library of Congress.

Cover illustrations by Art Glazer

Published by NTC LearningWorks
An imprint of NTC/Contemporary Publishing Company
4255 West Touhy Avenue, Lincolnwood (Chicago), Illinois 60646-1975 U.S.A.
Printed in the United States of America
International Standard Book Number: 0-8442-2476-6

18   17   16   15   14   13   12   11   10   9   8   7   6   5   4   3   2   1

Contents

About the Author

Deborah Perlmutter Bloch, Ph.D., is an associate professor of educational administration at Baruch College, the City University of New York. Previously she worked as both a high school counselor and English teacher, served as director of MetroGuide—New York City's computer-based career information delivery system—and acted as coordinator of research for the Office of Occupational and Career Education of the New York City Board of Education.

Dr. Bloch has consulted for national, state, and local organizations in areas related to career development, particularly the development and use of computerized career systems. She has been elected president of the National Career Development Association.

Acknowledgments

My thanks to all my friends and colleagues, and their friends and colleagues, who participated in the interviews for this book.

My husband, Martin, must again be thanked for his support, enthusiasm, and patience.

I would like to say a very special thank-you to my mother who has taught me more than I usually care to admit. Certainly, none of this would have been possible without her.

Author's Note: The names of all individuals and companies, the addresses and phone numbers used in examples, the sample resumes, and letters in this book are fictional.

Foreword

Three factors affect whether you will get the job for which you apply. Each has to do with how well you stack up in relation to your competitors, who are also trying their best to succeed in the same categories: (1) your "paper" qualifications, meaning the content and appearance of your application and/or resume; (2) what your references have to say about your performance and behavior while you worked for them; and (3) how you perform in your interviews.

In most cases, when an applicant is called in for an interview, he or she is considered qualified on the basis of the resume or application. You can't do much about what your references say about you. You are left with your final turn at bat, your chance to deliver a stellar performance when you are interviewed. If you have found that you don't perform as well in interviews as you would like, then it will pay you to work to improve your ability. You need to learn to make the most of whatever acting ability you have because in being interviewed, you, as a great many of us, are going to be relying upon learned behavior.

Through her extensive interviews with employers and recently hired employees in many different fields, and other data-gathering methods, Dr. Bloch has identified and distilled much valuable information. She writes crisply and succeeds in making this book "come alive" with down-to-earth, immediately useful information and advice.

This volume will become an outstanding and much-used addition to the resources of applicants, guidance and employment counselors, and libraries.

Catherine S. Lott
Former President
Nationwide Employment Service, Inc.

Oscar C. Lott
Former Employment Manager
E.I. du Pont Company

Editor's Note: The Lotts are the coauthors of *How to Land a Better Job*, VGM Career Horizons Series, Lincolnwood, Illinois, 1989, which was written from their combined experience of more than 50 years in top-level personnel positions in business, industry, and government.

Introduction

The National Alliance of Business and other forecasters have written about the anticipated differences in the nature of jobs by the year 2000. These differences will come about because of the shift from manufacturing to service industries, the growth of global and transnational commerce, and the increased use of automation. Because of these rapid economic changes, many of us will change jobs—and even occupations—more frequently than before. Getting a new job—the right new job—often depends on knowing how to have a winning interview.

This book is designed to help you learn and apply the twelve key steps to a winning interview. What is a winning interview? A winning interview is one that does two things for you. First, it helps you get the job for which you have applied. Second, it helps you figure out if the job for which you are interviewing is one you want. In other words, a winning interview produces a marriage between you and the potential employer.

How to Have a Winning Job Interview is based on many discussions with employers and recently hired employees in a variety of fields including banking, retail merchandising, fashion, computer science, advertising, education, and accounting. One of the most important ideas that came out of the discussions is that a winning interview is the result not only of what the candidate does during the interview, but what he or she has done before it.

Like any good performance, a winning interview requires preparation and rehearsal. This book includes many worksheets to help you prepare, rehearse, and perform. Be sure to use them. The twelve key steps to a winning interview are highlighted and explained so you can use them fully and confidently.

All of the recent employees reported that they had many job interviews before the winning one. The book, therefore, is also designed to help you understand and use the experiences from earlier interviews in later ones. It will help you improve your future performances based on realistic assessments of what you did that was right and wrong. The book will also help you learn from what your audience—the interviewer—said and did.

How to Have a Winning Job Interview is divided into three major sections: before, during, and after the interview. After the three sections, a special appendix is provided for a practice interview. You will need a willing friend to help you with this, but all the instructions for both of you are provided. At the end of the book, you will find a list of related readings to help you with all aspects of your job search.

Section I   Section I is called "Before the Interview." The five chapters in this section will help you prepare and rehearse for your interview.

Chapter 1, "Understanding the Purpose of Interviews," provides an overview of the expectations employers have of the interview process. Understanding their goals will improve both your preparation and the interview itself. At the same time, you need to analyze your own job requirements so that you can identify the information you want to gain in interviews. Of course, your overall goal is to get a job. However, you want it to be the best possible job for you so that you do not find yourself in the job-hunting process again too soon.

Chapter 2, is "Getting the Interview." In this chapter, you can review basic job-hunting techniques including how to look for a job and how to prepare a resume. You will also learn how to respond to an expression of interest from a prospective employer, and how to arrange the interview itself so that you have the information you need for the next steps.

Chapter 3, "Preparing: Your Brain," is about these next steps. In this chapter you learn how to get information about organizations and about yourself so that you are prepared for the kinds of questions you can expect to be asked in the interview.

Chapter 4, "Preparing: Your Body," helps you be certain you are dressed and groomed appropriately for the interview. One of the employers surveyed for this book said, "It should go without saying that cleanliness is essential, but don't write the book without saying it!"

Chapter 5, "Preparing: Your Emotions" gives you practical techniques for handling your feelings about the interview and for turning your nervous energy into positive energy. Throughout this section, you are provided with worksheets and checklists to make the general instructions personal and specific.

Section II   The next four chapters make up Section II, "During the Interview."

Chapter 6, "What to Expect," describes various interview formats and questions.

Chapter 7, "Giving Winning Answers," is about giving good answers and avoiding bad ones. You can see how to use the material you developed in the chapters in Section I so that you emphasize your strengths and minimize your weaknesses. You will also see some ways of dealing with illegal or inappropriate questions.

Chapter 8, "Asking Winning Questions," gives you advice on which questions to ask and, most important, when in the interview process to ask them. One of the most important issues in job hunting is salary. You will learn the best times and ways to discuss salary and other benefits.

Chapter 9, "Winning the Interview," concludes this section. It describes the subtle, and not so subtle, ways of behaving and responding that create favorable and unfavorable impressions. The chapter includes sound advice from the employers and the employees who had winning interviews.

Section III   Section III is called "After the Interview." It deals with two separate kinds of follow-up activities, one designed to maximize the results of your most recent interview and another for future interviews.

Chapter 10, "Maintaining Interest," shows you how to follow the interview with appropriate letters or telephone calls. The record-keeping system presented will enable you to remember key names, titles, dates, and results.

Chapter 11, "Experience Is the Best Teacher," will help you understand the process of the interview and use what you learned in future interviews.

Appendix A   Appendix A gives you the opportunity to practice your skills. You will need a willing partner, but all the steps for both of you to follow are clearly laid out.

Appendix B   Appendix B provides suggestions on useful additional reading.

BEFORE THE INTERVIEW

Section I

Understanding the Purpose of Interviews

1

Warning! Do not skip this chapter! You may be tempted to skip this chapter, to say, "I know why I'm going for an interview—to get a job." If that is what you said, or thought, then you have given an answer that is worth only 25 out of 100 points.

The answer to the question—"What is the purpose of an interview?"—is more complex. It has two sides: the employer's and the candidate's—yours. The major purpose of the interview is for the employer to select and hire the best possible person for the job. This is a very different answer from the sentence in the first paragraph. It changes the point of view from you to the employer. Picture a camera. If you say that the purpose of the interview is to get a job, you are the person holding the camera, deciding what will be in the picture, focusing the lens and taking the shot. However, when you understand that the purpose of the interview is for the employer to select the best employee, then you see that he or she is holding the camera and calling the shots. Of course, for the time of the interview, the camera is focused on you, and what you do during that period provides the picture the employer keeps.

In a winning interview, you will always have in the back of your mind the idea that it is the employer who invited you to the interview, who established the kind of interview it is, who selected the person or people who are interviewing you, and who has decided upon the criteria for judging candidates. It is the employer's show. However, for the duration of the interview, you are the star of that show.

Then there is the second purpose of the interview, which is to land a job. This is a good goal, but it is incomplete. The whole purpose of the interview, from your point of view, is to get you the job you want. This means that you will need to go into the interview knowing what you want in a job and knowing how to get information about the responsibilities and benefits that go with the job. You will also want to know how and when to gather the information so that the very act of asking the questions improves your chance of getting the job.

The question was: What is the purpose of the interview? The complete answer has two parts. The purpose of the job interview is: one—for the employer to select the best possible candidate, and two—for you to get the best possible job. In the first part of this chapter, the employers' purpose and their goals will be discussed. By learning more about how they see their goals and how they go about achieving them, you can understand more of what you need to bring to the interview. The second part of the chapter will help you identify some specific information-seeking goals for yourself. You will be working on the first two of the twelve key steps to a winning interview.

Key Step 1: Understand the employer's point of view.

The Employers' Goals

Employers in the fields of banking, accounting, education, fashion, computer science, and advertising were asked, "What is your goal in the interview?" Here are some of their answers:

"To find out something about the person—her background, interests, why she's interested in the job."

"To get a sense of how the person will fit into the organization. I already have his background written down in the resume. I want to know how he relates to others, how he deals with authority. Is he capable of independent decision making?"

"To hire people who are the best candidates."

"To find out if the candidate is qualified and to determine if the person will fit in socially as well as technically with the job environment. I also want to see if there are any people I know that I can call for recommendations."

"To find somebody who has the background and expertise for the level I seek and to convince them that we are the firm they want to join."

"To select the best person."

"To determine the capability, potential, and interest of the applicant. Is this person genuinely interested so we can keep her a reasonable period of time, or is she looking at our company because she was unsuccessful with her first or second choice?"

These answers give a few clues as to what employers are looking for. Of course, most of the statements are very broad, but there are a few useful hints to be gleaned from them. We can take key phrases from the statements and turn them into the questions that are in the back of these employers' minds when they conduct interviews.

Reading Employers' Minds

Employer's Phrase	Questions in Mind
the capability	When I put together everything I know about this person, can he do the job?
the potential	Every change of job or company brings some new responsibilities and a need for new ways of responding. Can she learn? Can she change?
genuine interest in the job	Does he want this job? Does he really want some other job? Does he understand his own needs and goals? Is he being honest about these with himself? With me?
genuine interest in the firm	Does he want to work for us? Is this just a quick stepping-stone job to another company?
background	Does she have the education, training, and experience for this job? Are the details of her schooling and work experience truthfully presented on the resume?
expertise	Does he have the specific skills and knowledge needed to carry out the job effectively and efficiently? What did he actually do in the jobs listed on his resume? How did he do in school?

Employer's Phrase	**Questions in Mind**
interests	Is this person balanced in her life? Does she have things she likes to do besides work? Will she usually be happy or depressed at work?
relates to others	Will he get along well with his co-workers? With customers? With people who report to him?
deals with authority	Will she get along well with me? Will she always be giving me or her immediate supervisor a hard time? Can she accept criticism? Can she take a "no" answer?
independent decision making	Can he think for himself? Can he act on what he thinks? Will he know when to act on his own and when to consult his boss?
fits in socially	Every company has its own way of doing things, of knowing when to be formal and when to be informal, of knowing whom to call only by last name, of knowing what has to be put in writing and what should never be put in writing. Will she be sensitive to these ways?
fits in technically	How do his skills and knowledge fit in with the skills of people we already have? Does he bring the skills that fill the gaps that we need filled?

Looking over the questions employers have in mind when they conduct interviews will help when you start to think of your background and how it will fit into the company and job for which you have applied. However, you can see that most of the questions in the employers' minds are not the questions that one actually asks during an interview. As an employer, I cannot say to you, "Are you sensitive? Do you know what you are doing?"

As an employer, I have to conduct an interview that will yield this information indirectly through your answers to my questions and through my questions back to you about your responses. The interview process is usually, therefore, somewhat loosely structured and consists of a give and take between the interviewer and the candidate.

Generally, the larger and more organized the company is, the more organized the interview may be. Bear in mind, however, that very few of the employers questioned had undergone any specific training in conducting interviews. Generally speaking, if you are interviewed by someone in the personnel department, that person has been trained in interview procedures. Her or his goal in the interview is usually to screen out people who don't have the needed background or who don't meet standards established for the job. You will often be interviewed by one person who holds a general managerial position and another who is the supervisor of the job in question. The goal of the general manager is to see how you will get along in the company. He or she is most interested in your ability to get along well with people. The goal of the supervisor of the job is to assess your technical and job-specific skills, and also to see how you will work with and fit in with the other people on the work team. Of course, many jobs are in small organizations where the manager and the supervisor are the same person and where there is no personnel department at all.

Some companies use rating sheets or systems to help them evaluate candidates. Whether the company to which you have applied uses a rating sheet or not, looking at some samples will help you zero in on the goals of the interview from the employer's perspective.

JOB CANDIDATE RATING SYSTEM: SAMPLE 1

Screening Questions

The following questions are suggested for employers' use in screening interviews. These questions are taken from the book *Hiring the Right Person for the Right Job*, by Dobrish, and others. The screening interview determines whether you will get to the next step, whether the door is still open for you in that company. The rating scale is outstanding, acceptable, or unacceptable, ending with an overall rating that says whether the candidate should be considered any further.

1. Does applicant have basic education for the job?
2. Does applicant have basic experience for the job?
3. Does applicant have special skills required for the job?
4. Can applicant meet special working conditions required?
5. Is grooming and general appearance adequate for job?
6. Does applicant show enthusiasm and interest in the work?
7. Does applicant communicate well? (Evaluate only if needed for job.)

The rating sheet might look something like this:

Screening Interview Rating Sheet

Job applied for: Applicant's name:

Interviewer: Address & phone:

Qualification	Outstanding	Acceptable	Unacceptable
1. ☐ Basic education			
2. ☐ Basic experience			
3. ☐ Special skills			
4. ☐ Can meet special working conditions			
5. ☐ Grooming & general appearance			
6. ☐ Enthusiasm & interest			
7. ☐ Communication necessary for job			

Additional comments:

Recommendation: Reject ☐   Call back for further interviewing ☐

JOB CANDIDATE RATING SYSTEM: SAMPLE 2

Personal Qualities

The same authors provide a "list of personal qualities essential to the performance of most technical, administrative, and professional jobs." The list includes:

Intelligence

Energy level

Maturity

Resourcefulness

Leadership

Assertiveness

Ability to work under direction

Attitudes

Communication ability

Personal Qualities Rating Sheet

Job applied for: Applicant's name:

Interviewer: Date of interview:

Quality	Excellent	Good	Fair	Poor
1. Intelligence				
2. Energy level				
3. Maturity				
4. Resourcefulness				
5. Leadership				
6. Assertiveness				
7. Ability to work under direction				
8. Attitudes				
9. Communication ability				
10. Overall rating				

JOB CANDIDATE RATING SYSTEM: SAMPLE 3

Personality, Motivation, and Character

In the book *The Evaluation Interview*, by Richard A. Fear, reports of interview findings are presented for employers to use as models. First, each report contains a narrative record of the candidate's work history, education and training, and present social adjustment. The section on present social adjustment includes comments on outside interests, friends, and general reactions to life. For each of these sections, the candidate is given a rating of above average, average, or below average. The fourth section of the report is called "Personality, Motivation, and Character." There are no comments given in this section, but the candidate is given one of the same three ratings—above average, average, or below average—on each of the characteristics listed in the motivation rating sheet below. The report concludes with a summary of assets, a summary of shortcomings, a general summary, and an overall rating.

Motivation Rating Sheet

Applicant's name   Interviewer's name

Characteristic	Above Average	Average	Below Average
1. Initiative			
2. Assertiveness			
3. Self-discipline			
4. Adaptability			
5. Tact			
6. Honesty and sincerity			
7. Perserverance			
8. Self-confidence			
9. Conscientiousness			
10. Hard work			
11. Teamwork			
12. Maturity			
13. Emotional adjustment			
14. Tough mindedness			

The sample rating sheets are not meant to frighten you out of going to the interview but to give you a sense of what employers are looking for. Remember that some employers have training in interview techniques. Furthermore, most of the qualities they are seeking are not easy to see in others. You go into the interview a step ahead if you understand that you are trying to show the employer not only what you know, but the best sides of your personality. In Section II of this book, you will see how employers' interview goals are translated into types of interviews and interview questions, and you will learn the winning techniques for answering these questions.

Key Step 2: Develop your own information goals.

Identifying Your Information Goals

Your first goal in the interview is, of course, to impress the employer more favorably than any other candidate so that you can get the job. Your second and related goal is to be sure that this is the best job for you at this time in your life and career. To meet this second goal, you need an understanding of what makes a specific job a good one for you. Just as it is the goal of employers to get information about you that they consider important, so it is your goal to get information about the job that you think is important. Your job requirements thus become your information goals.

Certainly before this point you have given some thought to what kind of work you want to do. You may be just out of school ready to go for your first job or perhaps well advanced in your career, but the very fact that you are reading this book means that you are in the job application process rather than at the job exploration stage. If you have little or no idea about the kind of job you should look for, then you need to take a step or two backwards. Things you might do to help you narrow your choices include:

- Go to the library and use the *Occupational Outlook Handbook* to read about various types of jobs.
- See a career counselor in your school, your company, your local state employment service, at a nearby university, or privately.
- Use a computer-based career information system available in many school districts and at local libraries.

- Read and work through a book about occupational choice such as *What Color Is Your Parachute?* by Richard Nelson Bolles or *How to Make the Right Career Moves* by Deborah Perlmutter Bloch.

Even though you have decided on the kind of work you want to do, or the job you are seeking, there are still questions to be answered about the organization in which you will work. Many jobs are available in a wide variety of industries. For example, if you are a word-processing machine operator, you can probably find work in just about any kind of organization you can imagine—public institutions, banks, large corporations, small companies, schools, hospitals, and even in companies that specialize in doing word processing on a job-by-job basis for others. If you are a nurse, you can certainly work in a hospital, but you can also look for work in one of the many large corporations that have personnel health departments. By carefully selecting the industry in which you apply for work, you may be able to combine your work skills and training with other strong interests you have.

On the following pages are twelve questions to ask yourself. These questions are about your own specific job requirements. They are, therefore, areas you will want to get information about during an interview. Your answers to the questions below form your information goals. They become, in essence, your rating sheet for a job. In Section II, "During the Interview," you will see how to translate your information goals into questions and at what point to ask the different kinds of questions during the interview process.

Information Goals Worksheet

Answer each question as completely and specifically as you can. If any question is about job requirements that are not important to you, draw a line through the blank answer space.

1. What kind of organization would I like to work for?
   (public or private, large or small, established or new, traditional or changing)

   _____

   _____

   _____

2. What kind of work schedule do I want?
   (regular or irregular hours, overtime, weekend work)

   _____

   _____

   _____

3. What kind of work setting do I want?
   (in the office all the time, in the field, a combination)

   _____

   _____

   _____

4. How much do I want to travel for work?

   _____

   _____

   _____

5. How willing, or eager, am I to relocate?

   _____

   _____

   _____

6. What is important to me about the geographical location of the job?
   (specific town, state or country, characteristics of climate)

_____

_____

_____

7. What salary range do I want?

_____

_____

_____

8. What other benefits are important to me?
   (medical plans, disability insurance, pension, profit sharing, vacation, education reimbursement)

_____

_____

_____

9. What is important to me about the personalities and attitudes of the people with whom I work?

_____

_____

_____

10. How much more education or formal training do I want?

_____

_____

_____

11. What are my career goals for five years from now?

_____

_____

_____

12. How do I expect the organization I am applying to now to contribute to those goals—do I hope
    to stay put or is this job a stepping-stone?

_____

_____

_____

Summary Worksheet

This chapter helped you see the purpose of the interview from the employer's point of view as well as your own. You saw how interviews move you one step further toward employment by enabling the prospective employer to get to know you better. Getting to know you includes checking the details of your resume, seeing if you will fill the company's needs, and seeing how you will fit in with the work style of the organization as well as with potential co-workers. You also developed your own list of job requirements which translate into interview goals so that you can use the interview process to get the information you need to make a wise decision about a job offer.

Use the statements below to review your understanding.

_____ I can see the interview from the employer's point of view. The employer wants:

_____

_____

_____ I can list the five qualities most employers would like to see in an employee. They are:

_____

_____

_____ I know what I want in a job. The most important things to me are:

_____

_____

_____ I understand my interview information goals. I must know:

_____

_____

Twelve Key Steps to a Winning Interview

In this chapter, you concentrated on:

Key Step 1: Understand the employer's point of view.
and
Key Step 2: Develop your own information goals.

Getting the Interview

This chapter is about how to get interviews and what to do in arranging the interview so that you can get the maximum benefit from your very first conversation with the prospective employer.

The interview is generally one of the last parts of the job-seeking process. Usually, the only thing that comes after the interview, or series of interviews, is the reference check. Therefore, it is important to take a look at the steps that lead up to and result in the interview.

This chapter has three parts. The first part is about general job-hunting techniques, the second is a brief overview of resume writing, and the third is about making arrangements for the interview.

Job-Hunting Techniques

There are four basic methods for seeking a job. There is no need for you to select only one method. A successful job campaign often includes the use of several or all of the methods. The four methods are:

- Networking

- Using professional employment services

- Answering advertisements

- Advertising yourself

Networking

Networking is a currently popular term that gives a technical sound to a technique that people have been using for a very long time. Basically, it means that you tell all the people you know that you are looking for a job and ask them to help you. Do not think that you don't know anybody. Think of the word *network.* Picture a network. It is not a single string from you to one person and from you to another person. It is like a web with strings from you to the people you know and from them to the people they know. People will generally like to help. One reason is because it makes them feel good. Another is because it may in turn increase their own network.

The first thing to do is to make a list of everyone you know. Consider people from all aspects of your life: family; friends; parents or children of friends; teachers; fellow members of religious, professional, and community organizations; sports teammates or opponents.

The next step is to think of what you want from each of these people—how each one can help you. Some may actually be employed by or run organizations in which you would like to work. Others may know people in the kinds of organizations you would like to work for. Still others may be just a shot in the dark. That is, you can't think of how they can help you, but it's worth seeing if they can. Your approach to each person may have to be a little different. You will be able to speak directly to some people when you see them in the course of everyday affairs. Others you may need to telephone or write.

Try to be as direct and specific as you can in your approach. One woman who wanted to change jobs knew many people in professional organizations. However, she saw them only once every few months at big national conferences. The first time, she said things like: "I'm really glad you like your job. If you hear of anything like it, let me know" and "I wish I could find a way to leave X (her current company)." What happened as a result of this? Nothing. The second time she saw her friends, she said the same kinds of things.

"I'm ready for a change." "I wonder what I'll be doing a year from now." What happened? Nothing. Finally, she said to one friend who told her about an impending promotion. "If you get that job, I would be interested in working for you in your former position." Her friend, to whom she had said the other weak statements, was surprised to hear she was job hunting! What happened? She was invited to apply for the job when her friend's promotion came through. She said to others, "I'm looking for a new job, and I'm willing to relocate anywhere from New England to Washington, D.C." Since they all knew the kind of work she did, they did not have to ask more. What happened? People she had not even spoken to directly—friends of friends, in other words—called her with suggestions and tips.

One of the most important techniques for a job search is keeping records of what you have done and where it has led. This is particularly important in networking since one contact may lead to another. Here is the kind of record you could keep for networking.

Networking Records

SAMPLE: Name <u>Paul Bishop</u>
Address <u>Ferry Road, Bristol, RI</u>
Telephone <u>(401) 555-2664 (work)</u>
Source of Contact <u>Friend of Aunt Lois</u>
Method of Contact <u>I telephoned him at work.</u>
Date(s) of Contact <u>2/17</u>
Results/Follow-up <u>He asked me to send him a resume.</u>
<u>Sent 2/19. Call him 2/28.</u>

CONTACT 1: Name _____

Address _____

Telephone _____

Source of Contact _____

Method of Contact _____

Date(s) of Contact _____

Results/Follow-up _____

_____

_____

CONTACT 2: Name _____

Address _____

Telephone _____

Source of Contact _____

Method of Contact _____

Date(s) of Contact _____

Results/Follow-up _____

_____

_____

CONTACT 3: Name _____

Address _____

Telephone _____

Source of Contact _____

Method of Contact _____

Date(s) of Contact _____

Results/Follow-up _____

_____

_____

CONTACT 4: Name _____

Address _____

Telephone _____

Source of Contact _____

Method of Contact _____

Date(s) of Contact _____

Results/Follow-up _____

_____

_____

CONTACT 5: Name _____

Address _____

Telephone _____

Source of Contact _____

Method of Contact _____

Date(s) of Contact _____

Results/Follow-up _____

_____

_____

Professional employment services

Professional employment services are available from a variety of sources. If you are in high school or college, your school probably has a placement office. If you have attended a college, you may be able to use the services of the placement office, often for a fee, even if you are no longer enrolled. State employment services also run employment offices. You can find these offices by looking under state listings in your local telephone directory. When you look at newspaper advertisements for jobs, you will see that many of them are placed by private employment agencies to which you can apply. Finally, there are private career consulting services.

Although all of the above agencies can be helpful to you in your job search, there are differences you should be aware of. The placement office in your school works for you. You are the customer whether the service is free or not. Their interest is in placing you in the best job they can. Employment agencies, on the other hand, work for companies with job vacancies. That is why there is no fee charged to you. The fee is paid by the hiring company. An employment agency's interest, therefore, is not in you but in finding the best possible person for the job. This does not mean they won't be helpful to you. What it does mean is that you need to know their point of view.

Some employment agencies which specialize in high-paying jobs are called "headhunters." They are usually interested only in highly experienced and qualified people. Therefore, if you are taking an unusual career path or just starting out, the "headhunter" type of agency will probably not be interested in you. Remember, it is not because you aren't qualified. It is because the agency is working for the employer.

State employment services are more neutral. Their goal is to make as many placements as possible so that fewer people are unemployed, and the economy of the state is healthy. The range of services provided by the state employment service varies from state to state.

The private career counseling services work for the client. However, many of these career counseling services do not provide job placement. Instead, they help you assess your goals and develop resume writing and interviewing skills, the kind of skills presented in this book and others like it.

Find the employment service most suited to your needs. Use it to identify job leads and to get any help offered in presenting yourself for a job. You need not stick to one choice. You can go to your school placement office, the state employment service, and register with several employment agencies.

Answering advertisements

Answering advertisements often leads to job interviews. You can find job advertisements in your local newspaper in the classified section and often in specialized sections for business, education, and health. Several major newspapers like the *New York Times* and the *Wall Street Journal* carry ads for national companies. If you are interested in working for a large organization, you might want to subscribe to one or both of these while you are job hunting. You will also find ads in professional newspapers and magazines. Of course, these are for jobs related to the interests of the readers. For example, *Computer World* lists programmer and analyst jobs.

Some advertisements call for a written answer. To answer such an ad, you will need to prepare your resume and write a cover letter. There is a brief summary of resume writing in this chapter, but you might want to use this book's companion, *How to Write a Winning Resume.*

Other advertisements ask that you call. The section at the end of this chapter, "Making Arrangements," gives helpful advice on making such calls.

Advertising yourself

Advertising yourself takes some time and a little bit of money but is often effective in getting a first job. There are two techniques you can use. First, you can actually take out an advertisement. The best place to do this is in a newspaper, magazine, or professional journal that reaches the audience that might want to hire you. It should be a magazine that has a "Situations Wanted" section as a regular part of its classified advertisements. Otherwise, no one may know to look for your ad. The second technique is to carry out a large distribution of your resume. You can locate the names for your resume mailing list through the classified telephone directory or a directory of business organizations such as *Standard & Poor's Register of Corporations, Directors and Executives.*

Resume Writing— A Brief Overview

There are many books about resume writing, so it would be silly to pretend that the whole subject could be covered as well in a few pages here. Of course, the recommended book is the companion to this book, *How to Write a Winning Resume.* However, if you already have a resume written and just want to be sure that it's good, the following overview will be helpful.

The method for writing a winning resume—a resume that gets you an interview—has five steps. The first step is to examine the relevant areas of your life in depth, making notes as you go. By writing out the details, you get the material that you need to write a comprehensive, convincing resume. Once you have written out the details, you then translate them into the best language for a resume. This language consists of action words (verbs) and a vocabulary related to the field of work in which you are job hunting. The third step is to select the parts of the resume you want to keep and write a draft. The fourth step is laying it all out, arranging it in the proper order on the page. The fifth step is a careful proofreading.

The possible sections of a resume, including those that are essential and those that are optional, are explained below. In addition, a good sample resume is given. Use the sections and their explanations to decide what should be in your resume. Use the sample resume as a model for your layout. In any case, your resume should be limited to one, or at most, two pages.

Resume sections

The heading is an essential section. It must include your name, home address, and telephone number. If you can receive calls at work, include your business number. This makes it easier for people to reach you during their business day.

Education is also an essential section. If you are an experienced worker, include the degrees you have earned, the institutions at which you earned them, and the dates of attendance. List your most advanced degree first. You should also list any courses taken to upgrade or enhance your skills. Finally, if you were awarded any honors in school, list them. No matter when you graduated, the honors are yours!

If you are not an experienced worker, then include any special course work or projects you have undertaken. Use these to show unusual accomplishment or energy. Do not list the regular courses of study for your field. The person reading the resume will probably regard that as an attempt to puff yourself up.

Work history is the most essential section and should include each of your jobs, beginning with the most recent. For each job, include the dates you worked, the company, and your title. List your major duties and responsibilities. Give more space to your more recent jobs. If you are just out of school, show your summer and part-time jobs even if they are not related to the job you are seeking. They show that you know how to work.

Professional licenses and certificates is an essential section if these are required for the kind of work you do. Give the title, issuing agency, and date of issuance for each license you hold.

Related experience is an optional section. It is helpful to have this section if you have work experience that is important to the job you are seeking, but that does not fit neatly into your work history. This might include experiences like consulting or teaching.

Professional association memberships and offices held is an optional section that should be included if you have significant accomplishments.

Leisure activities, like the optional section above, should be included only if you have activities that show enthusiasm, energy, and a high level of interest. These are characteristics employers like. However, if your hobbies are only of passing interest to you, do not include this section. When the potential employer starts to talk to you about them in the interview, your lack of real interest will count against you.

Special abilities is an optional section that you should include if you have abilities related to your work, such as knowledge of foreign languages. In general, these skills are listed after the work history. However, if you are looking for a job in the computer field, your knowledge of programming languages and computer systems should be the first item after the heading.

Publications and presentations should be included if you have any. If you believe the list will make your resume too long, make a statement within the resume, and attach a list at the end.

The job objective is definitely optional, and many employers prefer to see it explained in the cover letter. If you have a very specific job objective within a field, such as English teacher or business systems analyst, then you may want to include it. Definitely do not include a vague objective like, "a position which challenges my abilities and gives me the opportunity for growth." How many people are looking for boring, dead-end jobs?

Summary or highlights is neither an essential nor an optional section. All the employers surveyed for our previous publication *How to Write a Winning Resume* said they did not want this as part of a resume.

References is an optional section. Most employers do not expect to see these in a resume. If your references are on file with a school placement office, you may want to make a statement such as: References are available from: Placement Office, ABC University, 1234 5th Street, City, State, Zip.

Age, marital status, and physical characteristics make up the most controversial optional section. It is now against the law for companies to discriminate on the basis of this information, and some employers are uncomfortable when they see it. Others like to see it to get a picture of the person they are reading about and to see whether "the person will fit into a group of people I already have."

What should you do? Your goal is to write a winning resume. If you believe that your personal characteristics are right on target for the job you are seeking, include them. If you have any doubts, leave them out.

The following is a sample resume of a young man who is seeking his second job as a programmer.

Resume

Michael Faber

118-27 221 Street
Jamaica, New York 11411

Home (718) 555-7661
Work (212) 555-1234

EDUCATION

State University of New York at Buffalo, B.A., 1990, Major: Computer Science, Minor: Mathematics
Brooklyn Polytechnic Institute, National Science Foundation program, Summer, 1987, "Dynamic Modeling"

COMPUTER SKILLS

Languages: Proficient in Pascal, BASIC
Familiar with C, Fortran, Assembler, Cobol

Operating Systems: Proficient in MS/DOS, VM/CMS, UNIX, RSTS, CP/M

Machines: IBM 360/370, IBM PC/XT, PDP 11/70, VAX 11,
Data General NOVA, Apple, Wang 600

WORK EXPERIENCE

1990–present PROGRAMMER

Laser and Beam, Inc.
New York, New York

Develop and improve special needs programs for accounting companies using MS/DOS and UNIX based microcomputers. Write technical and user documentation. Participate in the training of end users who have little or no computer expertise.

1988–1989 COMPUTER SPECIALIST
(summers)

Association of Youth
Technical Clubs in Israel
Haifa, Israel

Managed microcomputer laboratory. Programmed database for office filing system. Taught Pascal and BASIC to high school age students.

1985–1986 SALESCLERK
(part-time)

Doowah Record Store
Jamaica, New York

OTHER ACTIVITIES

Active member IBM PC User Group

> **Key Step 3:** Get all the interview appointment information you need.

Making Arrangements

You are now up to the stage where you are ready to make arrangements. This means you have inspired enough interest in a potential employer so that he or she is willing to spend some time with you. You may have done this through networking contacts, through referral by an employment service of one type or another, or by writing in answer to an advertisement or some other type of lead.

Generally speaking you will receive a telephone call from a member of the personnel department or from a secretary representing the person who will interview you. Sometimes you will get a letter asking you to telephone, and sometimes you will get a letter asking you to come at a specific time. This second kind of letter usually means that you are going to be interviewed by a panel of people in a structured situation. The structured interview and other styles of interviewing will be discussed in Section II, "During the Interview."

As soon as you send out your first resume or make your first contact, you should be ready to accept an invitation to an interview. To do this, you need to think about the information you will need to get to the right place, at the right time, prepared to do your best.

What is the absolute minimum information you need?

- the name of the company
- the street address of the company
- travel directions
- the name of the person you are going to see
- the room number of that person
- the date and time of the interview
- the name of the person to whom you are speaking
- the telephone number of that person

What other information is it helpful to have?

- the title or position of the person you are going to see
- other people who will be present at the interview
- their titles or positions
- materials or samples of work to bring with you

You are also going to need quite a bit of information about the organization. Techniques for getting this information are discussed in the next chapter, "Preparing: Your Brain." Since you can sometimes get some of the information from the organization itself, read the chapter as soon as you can.

In many cases, the person who will interview you is not part of a personnel department, and the secretary calling you is not particularly familiar with making arrangements for an employment interview. You must take the responsibility for getting the information you need.

It is often so exciting when the call for an interview comes that it is difficult to remember all your needs during the call. But you must! Keep the following interview arrangements worksheets handy, and use them when you get the call. Make more copies if you need them. If you think you might get some calls at work as well as at home, keep copies in both places. Be sure you have all the spellings and pronunciations correct before you hang up. Remember, it is better to ask to have something repeated than to go into the interview calling Mr. Baily, "Mr. Quaily."

Interview Arrangements Worksheet 1

Name of Organization _____

Street Address _____

Room Number _____

Date _____

Travel Directions _____

_____

Name of Interviewer _____

Title of Interviewer _____

Others to be at the Interview: Names and Titles

_____

_____

_____

Person Making Arrangements _____

Telephone Number _____

Materials to Bring _____

Additional Notes _____

_____

_____

_____

_____

_____

Interview Arrangements Worksheet 2

Name of Organization _____

Street Address _____

Room Number _____

Date _____

Travel Directions _____

_____

Name of Interviewer _____

Title of Interviewer _____

Others to be at the Interview: Names and Titles

_____

_____

_____

Person Making Arrangements _____

Telephone Number _____

Materials to Bring _____

Additional Notes _____

_____

_____

_____

_____

Summary Worksheet

This chapter helped you identify some job-hunting methods including networking, using employment services, answering advertisements, and advertising yourself. Basic resume-writing techniques were also reviewed. All of these lead to making arrangements for interviews. You were able to see the kind of basic information you must get when you first arrange for the interview. Two worksheets, one for keeping track of network contacts and one for making interview arrangements, were included in this chapter.

Review your skills.

_____ I know how to use a variety of job-hunting sources. They are:

_____

_____

_____

_____

_____ I have prepared a winning resume. I have checked my resume for the following:

_____

_____

_____

_____

_____ I am ready to get all the information I need when I arrange for a job interview. It includes:

_____

_____

_____

_____

Twelve Key Steps to a Winning Interview

In this chapter you concentrated on

Key Step 3: Get all the interview information you need.

Preparing: Your Brain

This chapter will help you get your thoughts and ideas together in preparation for the interview. The goal is to have the information you need before you go into the interview. While you do not want to rehearse your answers and have them sound memorized, you do want to sound intelligent, interested, and knowledgeable. Very often you will not have much time between being called for an interview and the interview itself. Therefore, it is a good idea to work through some ideas as soon as you apply for a job.

Remember that in Chapter 1, "Understanding the Purpose of Interviews," you saw that employers are looking for people with capability, potential, expertise, interest, the ability to think, and the ability to get along well with others. Just as employers cannot learn anything by directly asking the questions in the back of their minds, you cannot communicate the qualities they are seeking simply by saying you have them. It would not do an employer any good to ask, "Do other people like you?" Similarly, you cannot say, "I really work and get along well with others," and have that sentence communicate the idea. You need to use the facts of your experience and background and your knowledge of the job and the organization to communicate your skills and strengths.

To prepare for this kind of communication, there are three steps to carry out:

1. Assess your own strengths and knowledge as shown by your experience, education, and other interests and activities. Methods for doing this step are in the first part of this chapter called "Assessing Your Strengths."

2. Examine the responsibilities of the job you are seeking, and match your skills to these needs. Methods for doing this step are in the second part of this chapter called, "Job Match."

3. Learn what you can about the organization or industry, and see how you can contribute to that organization. Methods for doing this are in the third part of this chapter, "Organizational Fit."

Of course, you can expect to go for more than one interview. The experience of recently hired employees shows that they interviewed for between fifteen and thirty jobs before they had the winning interview. Some of the preparation you do will be useful for all interviews. Some, like the research on the organization, will have to be repeated for each prospective employer you expect to see.

Key Step 4: Assess your own strengths and weaknesses.

Assessing Your Strengths   For this part of the interview preparation, you need to think about your own strengths. To do this you will need to be honest with yourself. While some people exaggerate their own abilities, many others tend to be overly modest. The important thing here is to take a good hard look at yourself and be as fair to yourself as you would be to a stranger.

On the following pages are a series of questions with plenty of space to answer them. The directions are simple. Answer the questions. If any of the questions don't apply to your background or your job, skip them.

Strength Assessment Worksheet 1

What job skills have you acquired through education or training?

Skill	Program, Course, or Other Source
EXAMPLE: Type 60 wpm	High school typing—one year
_____	_____
_____	_____
_____	_____
_____	_____

What job skills have you acquired on the job?

Skill	Job Responsibility
EXAMPLE: Able to defuse anger	Handled customer complaints
_____	_____
_____	_____
_____	_____

What were the most important duties on your most recent job and what skill did you need to carry out each task?

Duty	Skill
EXAMPLE: Contacted field offices to identify problems	Able to get people to speak openly
_____	_____
_____	_____
_____	_____
_____	_____

Strength Assessment Worksheet 2

Listed below are 10 personal traits. Put a check next to each one that is true of you, and describe how you used that trait on a recent job or, if this is only your first or second job, how you used each trait in some other area of activity.

Trait	Activity
_____ 1. Team worker	_____
	_____
	_____
	_____
	_____
_____ 2. Tactful	_____
	_____
	_____
	_____
	_____
_____ 3. Adaptable to change	_____
	_____
	_____
	_____
	_____
_____ 4. Have initiative	_____
	_____
	_____
	_____
	_____
_____ 5. Self-disciplined	_____
	_____
	_____
	_____
	_____

_____ 6. Conscientious

_____

_____

_____

_____

_____

_____ 7. Hard worker

_____

_____

_____

_____

_____

_____ 8. Honest and sincere

_____

_____

_____

_____

_____

_____ 9. Intelligent

_____

_____

_____

_____

_____10. Self-motivated

_____

_____

_____

_____

Strength Assessment Worksheet 3

You probably said on your resume that "references are available." There is a good chance you will be asked for them during the interview. List both work and character references below. Be sure you know how to spell all the names and know how references can be reached by telephone during the business day and by mail.

Reference & Organization	Address (with Zip)	Telephone
Example		
Margaret Henry	5555 Western Blvd.	(555) 555-5555
Director of Marketing	Hobart, Wyoming	
Hobart Manufacturing Co.	55555	

Strength Assessment Worksheet 4

What do you consider to be your three greatest weaknesses, and how are you working to overcome them? (Knowing your weaknesses, not pretending you are Superman or Wonder Woman, helps you identify your strengths.)

Example of a Weakness: Being a know-it-all

I can overcome it by: Trying harder to listen to others

Weakness 1: _____
_____
_____

I can overcome it by: _____
_____
_____
_____
_____

Weakness 2: _____
_____
_____

I can overcome it by: _____
_____
_____
_____

Weakness 3: _____
_____
_____

I can overcome it by: _____
_____
_____
_____
_____

Key Step 5: Learn all you can about the job and organization.

Job Match   This part of the chapter will help you see how your skills and strengths match the requirements of the job you are seeking.

You will want to have information about the formal training you need for the job, the technical skills or expertise required, and the kind of interpersonal skills needed. For example, if you are applying for a job as a restaurant manager, a two- or four-year degree in restaurant management might be required. Technical skills would include a knowledge of health and safety rules, of equipment and food purchasing, of menu planning, of record keeping, of staff hiring and training, and of customer relations. Interpersonal skills would include the ability to communicate with a wide variety of people, to organize and direct activities, and to work under pressure.

There are a number of excellent sources of information about jobs. First, you are a source. If you are applying for a job, you probably know something about it. Perhaps it is the same or similar to the job you already have. Other people you may know in similar jobs are another source. Speak to them about the jobs they are doing. If you are working with an employment service of any of the types described in chapter 2, you should be able to get information from them. If you answered an advertisement for a job, the ad itself probably contains information about the requirements. Many organizations, particularly large ones, have written job descriptions. Write or call the personnel department for a copy.

If none of the specific sources above work, your local library can be of help. Some libraries have access to computer-based career information systems. From the system you can get job descriptions and information about how to prepare for a job. The *Occupational Outlook Handbook* is another reliable source of information. In addition, your library may have files of bulletins or brochures about different occupations.

This chapter includes three "Job Match Worksheets," one for educational requirements, one for technical skills, and one for interpersonal skills. Each worksheet has one column for the job requirements, one column for the abilities you have to meet those requirements, and a third column for the experience you have had that proves or documents your abilities. Fill in the first column on each of the worksheets as you do your research.

Key Step 6: Match your skills to the job requirements.

After you have completed the columns of job requirements, use the first part of this chapter to help trigger your thoughts for the second and third columns. Employers are most interested in directly related work experience. But if you do not have that, be sure to think about other activities in your life that are relevant to the requirements. Be sure to include information that documents your skill and knowledge. These experiences provide the meat for your interview. They enable you to express your strengths in concrete ways.

If you are applying for jobs that are different from each other, you may want to copy these sheets before you begin so that you can prepare different sheets for different jobs.

Job Match Worksheet 1—Educational Requirements

Job Title _____

Name of Organization _____

Job Requirement	My Qualifications	Proof
EXAMPLE: *Degree in Accounting*	*B.S. Accounting Major*	*Syracuse Univ. 1991*

Job Match Worksheet 2—Technical Skills

Job Title _____

Name of Organization _____

Job Requirement	**My Qualifications**	**Proof**
EXAMPLE: *Able to project budgets*	*Prepared budgets for school district's grant applications*	*Ass't. coordinator of planning, Hillsdale School District, 1989–1991*

Job Match Worksheet 3—Interpersonal Skills

Job Title _____

Name of Organization _____

Job Requirement	**My Qualifications**	**Proof**
EXAMPLE: Able to deal with a variety of people	Handled customer complaints	Ass't. to sales manager, ACME Manufact'g. 1988–1990

Organizational Fit   Not only is it important for you to know about the job you are seeking, but knowing about the company or organization that is interviewing you is also important. All of the recently hired people said that part of their success was due to their researching the company or industry. As one moves into professional, supervisory, or managerial positions, this research becomes more and more important.

Many of the sources of information about jobs are also sources of information about organizations. If you are already employed by the company and changing jobs, you, yourself, are a source. Stop and think of what you know not just about your job, but about the organization for which you work. You may know other people already employed by the company. Speak to them, being careful to get information and not biases. Again, if you are working with an employment service, they should be able to help you.

Large corporations maintain public relations departments, and you can ask that department for any pamphlets about the company. You may not even have to tell them that you are looking for work there. Public corporations must file annual reports. These are available to stockholders and can also be found in business libraries. Recent newspapers and magazines may have run articles about particular companies or industries. If you have not come across any, you can use the index to *The New York Times* or other newspapers and magazines for current information.

There are also a number of directories that have specific information about company assets, revenues, and personnel. Some of these are:

- *Dun and Bradstreet's Million Dollar Directory*

- *Standard & Poor's Register of Corporations, Directors and Executives*

- *Standard Directory of Advertisers*

You will find these and other directories in your library.

When you are called for an interview, you may sometimes be able to ask whether there is someone in the organization you can speak to for further information. Generally, this request is better received in public organizations such as schools rather than in business companies.

Thinking about the organization to which you have applied will help you understand how you are going to fit in and even something of the nature of the work you may be expected to do. For example, in a smaller business you may have varied responsibility and tasks, since with fewer people each one may wear many hats.

On the other hand, in a larger organization work tends to be more specialized, and knowing the organization can help you anticipate some questions you may be asked. You need to know not only information about your own job, but how that job relates to the products, services, and customers or clients of the organization.

For example, if you are applying for a job as an office worker in a pharmaceutical company, you want to be able to show your knowledge of the vocabulary of that field. While the basics of office work may be the same as if you were applying to an insurance company, the lingo will be different.

Finally, knowledge of the organization can help you frame winning rather than losing answers. If you have, for example, applied for a job in a school—as a teacher, dietitian, custodial worker, bus driver, or secretary—you want to talk about students or pupils, rather than calling them customers or kids.

The worksheets that follow are designed to help you think about the organization that is going to interview you and about how you would fit into that organization. This is not information that you are going to recite during the interview. It is information that will help you in formulating answers to the questions you are asked.

Since you will probably apply to more than one organization, it is a good idea to make copies of these worksheets before you begin.

Organizational Fit—Worksheet 1

Job Title: _____

Name of Organization: _____

What is the major product or service of this organization?

_____
_____
_____
_____

How does the job I am seeking contribute to the product or service?

_____
_____
_____
_____

How is the company or institution organized?

_____
_____
_____
_____

What would my position be within the organization?

_____
_____
_____
_____

How will my position in the organization be similar to or different from previous positions I have held?

_____
_____
_____
_____

Organizational Fit—Worksheet 2

What are some of the goals of the organization or of the industry at large?

_____

_____

_____

_____

_____

_____

_____

_____

_____

_____

How can my skills contribute to reaching these goals?

_____

_____

_____

_____

_____

_____

_____

_____

_____

_____

_____

Organizational Fit—Worksheet 3

What are some of the issues, concerns, or problems in this organization or industry?

_____

_____

_____

_____

_____

How can I contribute to the solution?

_____

_____

_____

_____

What are some of the changes in the industry or workplace that can be expected in the next five years?

_____

_____

_____

_____

How will I adapt to those changes?

_____

_____

_____

_____

_____

Summary Worksheet

This chapter helped you identify your strengths and skills and to see how they will fit in with the job or jobs for which you will be interviewed. It also gave you some questions to think about for the organizations that will be interviewing you and some sources of information. In later chapters you will see how to use the information in the worksheets to produce winning interviews. Since this chapter was filled with worksheets analyzing your strengths, it seems appropriate that it end with one.

SUMMARY OF STRENGTHS

Listed below are five reasons why any employer would be foolish *not* to hire me!

1. _____

_____

2. _____

_____

3. _____

_____

4. _____

_____

5. _____

_____

Twelve Key Steps to a Winning Interview

In this chapter you concentrated on

Key Step 4: Assess your own strengths and weaknesses.

Key Step 5: Learn all you can about the job and organization.   and

Key Step 6: Match your skills to the job requirements.

Preparing: Your Body

The first impression the interviewer, your potential employer, will have of you is a visual one. That impression must be used to prepare her or him to listen to you. The book *Deciphering the Senses* is about how people get and use information from the world around them. The authors of that book write, "These signs and signals of the visual language of the body all obviously take advantage of the fact that, for most humans, 'seeing is believing.' Despite the importance of the other senses to survival . . . , humans tend to trust information conveyed by the eyes above data provided by any of the other senses."

What is there in appearance that commands a listener's attention, that makes a person want to listen to you? First and most basic is good grooming. Good grooming translates into cleanliness and neatness. Second is the choice of clothes. People tend to feel most comfortable with people who are similar to themselves. This translates into choosing

51

clothes that reflect a knowledge of the job for which you are applying. Finally, the kind of attention you want to attract in a job interview is attention to your mind and work skills. That translates into avoiding striking accessories.

There are three parts to this chapter: good grooming, choosing clothes, and selecting appropriate accessories. The point of this chapter, and of this entire book, is to help you have a winning interview. The suggestions made are directed toward that goal rather than toward self-expression or other goals that you might have in dressing for other occasions.

Key Step 7: Plan how you will look as carefully as you plan what to say.

Good Grooming

All of the employers interviewed said, "Neatness counts!" or words to that effect. It is essential that your appearance in the interview show that you know how to take care of your hair, your teeth, your hands, and your body. An employer will find it difficult to hire someone to take care of a job who has not learned how to take care of herself or himself.

Your hair should be neatly and attractively cut and freshly washed. If you have a problem with dandruff, ask your pharmacist to help you select a special shampoo.

If you are looking for a job in a very traditional industry such as banking or accounting, you may want to get a very conservative haircut. In any case, this is not the time to try the very latest style. Remember, you are trying to get interviewers to pay attention to your ideas, not your looks.

The authors of *Deciphering the Senses* describe people as "human semaphores." That means we send signals not only by what we say, but by how we look. "Every part of the body is involved," they write. "Since the first visual contact made with others is generally with the face and head, hair is of vital importance. It immediately identifies male or female, while giving plenty of opportunity for individual expression of the person's relationship to (or lack of concern for) peers and the general cultural values."

Clean teeth are the result of good, ongoing dental care. If you do not have clean teeth, you probably have bad breath. If you have bad breath, interviewers will spend their energy avoiding inhaling rather than listening to what you have to say.

See your dentist to be sure your teeth are in healthy condition. Clean your teeth daily with dental floss. Brush your teeth twice a day. Many dentists recommend that at least one brushing a day be done with baking soda and peroxide. Be sure to brush your teeth thoroughly before leaving for the interview.

Bad breath can also be caused by eating a lot of garlic or raw onions. Some people retain the odors from these foods long after eating them. Your best bet is to avoid dishes with a lot of garlic and any raw onions on the day of an interview.

Sometimes, in spite of best efforts, a person has bad breath. If you have this problem, suck on a mint candy or chew a piece of gum just before going for the interview. Be sure to get rid of the candy or gum before going into the building in which the interview will take place. All of the employers surveyed said that gum chewing during the interview was unforgivable.

Hands must be clean with manicured fingernails. This does not mean you need to get a professional manicure. It does mean that your nails should be evenly cut and smooth. Use an emery board or nail file to smooth jagged edges. Clean under your nails with a nail brush. Use an orange stick or the point of a nail file to get out stubborn pieces of dirt. These tools are inexpensive and available in every drugstore.

Many people, including the recently hired employees who were interviewed, favor a really conservative approach to appearance at an interview. That style is never wrong. Women, following the conservative approach, will use a pale pink or natural colored nail polish. Men will have unpolished nails.

Your body must also be clean. Be sure to shower or bathe the day of the interview. Use deodorant. If you tend to have a heavy body odor, use one of the deodorants designed for that purpose. Again, check with your druggist.

Choosing Clothes

The clothes that you wear to the interview should reflect your understanding of the job, contribute to your own good feelings, and help you look your best.

How can clothes reflect an understanding of the job? Ask yourself this question: Do people who hold jobs similar to this one usually wear suits to work?

If the answer is "yes," then, if you are a man, you should wear a suit (with a shirt and tie) to the interview. Your shoes, lace-ups or slip-ons, should be comparably formal in style. Do not wear sneakers or very casual moccasins with a suit.

If the answer is "yes," and you are a woman, then you should wear a business suit, tailored blouse, and pumps. Think about the company for which you are interviewing, and the industry into which it fits. The more traditional the company or industry, the more conservative your clothes should be. One employer, a banker, said that although he had many suits to wear to work, they all looked alike. Each one was gray and traditional in cut.

If the answer is "No, people do not usually wear suits to work on this job," then you have somewhat more freedom in how you dress for the interview. Of course, you may choose to wear a suit. On the other hand, if you are a man, you could choose a sportcoat, shirt, tie, and slacks. You might wear a shirt, tie, slacks, and sweater. If you are a woman, you can choose a skirt and blouse or a tailored dress. Again, sneakers or very casual shoes are not appropriate.

The clothes you choose should also make you feel good about yourself. Most people have some clothes in which they feel more cheerful, happier within themselves. This may be because of the color of the clothes, the way they fit, or their texture. Try to pick clothes that give you this good feeling.

The clothes you wear to the interview must be clean and well pressed. It is a good idea to have your clothes dry-cleaned or washed just before wearing them to the interview even if you might have gotten another wearing out of them without it. This way you are sure that there are no spots or lingering body odors.

Appropriate Accessories

Although women tend to use more kinds of accessories than men, both women and men wear jewelry and use scent. The key word for men and women in all accessories for the interview is *moderation.*

If you wear jewelry—rings, bracelets, earrings, tie clips, pins, necklaces—wear just enough to enhance your appearance. Generally speaking, more than one ring per hand is excessive. Bracelets can distract from an interview by making noise or getting caught in something. It's a good idea to avoid them. Remember, you do not want to draw attention to some ornament like your favorite large, single, party-purple feather earring. On this occasion, you want all the attention to focus on you.

A light scent, lightly applied as aftershave lotion, cologne, toilet water, or perfume can also help you feel good and smell good. Remember your goal is not to daze the interviewer with a heady cloud of perfume, but to create a pleasant feeling within yourself.

If you are going to carry a handbag or briefcase, it should be businesslike and complement the outfit you are wearing. If you are a man you will want to avoid handbags, as they are still considered to be unusual for men in America.

You will be bringing with you a copy of your resume, any materials you were asked to bring, and your notes on references. Use a briefcase or, if that is not appropriate to your business, a plain manilla envelope. Avoid arriving at an interview with shopping bags, bundles or boxes, or with the papers you will need stuffed into your handbag or pockets. If you are a woman and you carry an ample-sized tailored-style purse, you may be able to carry your papers that way. The important thing is to be comfortably organized, with your papers neatly available.

One of the employers interviewed for this book said, "A person should look well-groomed. Conservative dress appeals to me. If someone comes in, say, in a shirt with loud stripes, I turn it around. I think if I were going to an interview, I wouldn't know who I was going to meet. I wouldn't want to offend them. If someone isn't aware of that idea, I wonder why. It distracts me from the interview."

A 1990 *New York Times* article on job seeking during an economic downturn quoted a successful job seeker, "I paid attention to a lot of little things. I used engraved stationery. I lost 30 pounds. I shined my shoes once a day. I had a haircut every week. If you know you're looking your best and feeling your best, it helps put you in an 'up' mood."

Summary Worksheet

The purpose of this chapter has been to help you prepare your appearance for an interview. Use the checklist below to help you remember what to do.

_____ I brush my teeth regularly.

_____ My hands are clean with well-manicured nails.

_____ My hair is freshly cut and clean.

_____ I have found the best deodorant.

_____ I have chosen clothes that go with the job and make me feel good.

_____ I have had my clothes cleaned.

_____ I have selected a small amount of jewelry.

_____ I have selected a light scent and used just a little.

_____ I have a briefcase or envelope to carry my papers.

Twelve Key Steps to a Winning Interview

In this chapter you concentrated on

Key Step 7: Plan how you will look as carefully as you plan what to say.

Preparing:
Your Emotions

Every single person surveyed for this book said that he or she felt nervous before the interview. Many of the employers, on the other hand, said that they looked for a certain amount of self-assuredness and confidence. This chapter is not about eliminating nervousness. To some extent, nervousness means your body is getting ready for some test of strength; your juices are flowing. This chapter is about controlling nervousness and turning that nervous energy into positive energy.

We asked some successful employees how they dealt with nervousness, what they did to help themselves feel good before an interview. Here are some of their answers:

"I know I need rest. I need to relax physically. The day before an interview, I didn't run from my job to shop in a department store. I went home, read the paper, and got a good night's sleep."

"I leave myself just enough time to get to the interview so that I just focus on getting there. Then I walk to the interview. That gets rid of a lot of tension."

"I go through a lot of normal stuff like before a test. I try to plan the interview in my mind, think of the questions I might be asked. Also dressing well makes me feel confident."

"I rely on thinking of the actor's saying. It's something like, 'If you're nervous before you go on stage, you won't be nervous on stage, and if you're not nervous before you go on stage, you're in trouble.' I really just let the nervousness happen. All the nervousness beforehand gets you prepared, psyched."

"I use a little meditation and visualization. I picture myself being calm and having an easy, flowing conversation with another human being."

You may have your own ways of reducing and controlling nervousness. In this chapter you will see three techniques, each of which can be used alone or in combination with the others. One of these is a method of relaxation for stress reduction. In this method, you actually use controls over your body to stop the physical signs of nervousness. The second method is visualization. In this, you create pictures in your mind of how you want the interview to go. The third method, rational thinking, helps you eliminate irrational, negative thoughts. Each of these methods is based on the work and writing of many people. References to their books will enable you to read more about any of the methods that interest you.

> **Key Step 8:** Turn nervous energy into positive energy through relaxation, visualization, and rational thinking.

Relaxation Nothing can be more annoying when you are nervous than having someone say, "Just relax!" Try as you may, you cannot do it. In fact, often the harder you try, the more nervous you become. This section will show you some techniques that can help you overcome nervousness. However, they are not very useful if you use them only when you are already upset. They work best if you practice and apply them regularly.

The feeling of nervousness with its sweaty palms, twisting stomach, and cold feet is actually a physical response to what the mind perceives as danger. This response, called "flight or fight," is appropriate if we are facing an immediate physical danger. It gets the body ready to protect itself. However, our brain cannot distinguish between an immediate physical danger, such as facing a ferocious bear, and a more psychological (and common) danger, such as facing an unknown interviewer. Since it is obviously not desirable that you go into the interview ready to take on the interviewer with your bare hands or ready to run away as fast as you can, teaching yourself a relaxation technique is helpful for this and other stressful situations in life.

If you are familiar with any forms of meditation, you will see that the relaxation techniques described in this section draw heavily on what can be learned from these ancient practices. Some forms of meditation are associated with religious or philosophical beliefs, but it is not necessary to subscribe to any particular set of beliefs to benefit from relaxation exercises.

Relaxation training is used in many fields to help people improve their lives. In *Mind as Healer, Mind as Slayer,* Kenneth R. Pelletier describes how relaxation can help you improve your health, not just during the moments when you are relaxing, but as a long-term benefit. The technique in Relaxation Exercise 1 is one that he describes.

One of the best books to describe the techniques of relaxation and how they can benefit you is *Relaxation Response* by Herbert Benson. Many of the same techniques are used in yoga and other meditative disciplines. *The Meditative Mind* by Daniel Goleman provides an interesting introduction to various meditative practices.

Relaxation Exercise 1

Choose a quiet place with soft light, good ventilation, and a comfortable temperature. Try to make sure that you will not be interrupted by anyone's arrival, the telephone, your housepets, or any other distractions. Make yourself comfortable either sitting on the floor, or in a straight-backed chair, where you can sit erect without strain. Sit cross-legged or, if using a chair, with your feet planted firmly on the floor.

Once you have made yourself comfortable, close your eyes and, breathing evenly, free your mind of any nagging worries or task-oriented thoughts. Concentrate on a sound, a mood, or a place of natural beauty that has given you a sense of peace. Relax in this position for 15 or 20 minutes a day, and allow your thoughts to flow freely, without trying to force them into any pattern or direction.

If you wish, jot down thoughts below of sounds, moods, places that have been relaxing to you in the past and that evoke a sense of peace or meditative mood in you as you remember them.

_____

_____

_____

_____

_____

_____

_____

_____

_____

_____

_____

_____

_____

_____

Relaxation Exercise 2

Another book which suggests the use of relaxation training is *Quantum Fitness* by Irving Dardik and Denis Waitley. Dardik and Waitley suggest the use of a method called "autogenic training" to help gain the maximum benefits from a healthy diet and exercise program. You can use it to gain a more productive interview. Here is the technique they suggest.

First there are six sentences to learn. Once you have learned them, you will use them in repetitions. The sentences are:

1. My arms and legs are heavy.

2. My arms and legs are heavy and warm.

3. My heartbeat is calm and regular.

4. My breathing is relaxed and effortless.

5. My stomach is warm.

6. My forehead is cool.

Now, sit in a quiet place in a chair with good back support or lie on a bed or carpeted floor with your arms at your sides. You are now ready to repeat your sentences, paying attention to what you are saying and letting it occupy your mind and your body. Close your eyes, take a few deep, regular breaths and begin.

1. Start with your right arm if you are right handed and say: "My right arm is heavy. I am at peace. My right arm is heavy. I'm relaxing. My right arm is heavy." (Repeat the sentences for your left arm, for both your arms, for your right leg, for your left leg, and for both your legs.)

2. Start with the same arm and say: "My right arm is heavy and warm. I am at peace. My right arm is heavy and warm. I am relaxing. My right arm is heavy and warm." (Repeat the sentences for your left arm, for both your arms, for your right leg, for your left leg, and for both your legs.)

3. Repeat the next key sentence, "My heartbeat is calm and regular," ten times. Do the same with the sentences about breathing, about your stomach, and about your forehead.

4. Keeping your eyes closed, extend your arms in front of you. Take a deep breath. Flex your arms, and let your breath out. Let your arms relax. Open your eyes.

There are many other relaxation techniques. The books mentioned throughout this chapter as well as others listed at the end of this book describe these techniques and give directions for practicing them. What is important is not what technique you choose, but that you use it regularly.

Visualization

Another way you can help yourself is by using the energy within you to visualize the outcome you want. You can do this by projecting yourself into the interview situation and picturing yourself having a winning interview. How you think about a situation or event affects the outcome of that event.

Some people believe that this happens because you psychologically influence the outcome. Often when negative outcomes are feared and then happen, it is called a self-fulfilling prophecy. If you feel you will act poorly in an interview, you make yourself more frightened, you cannot marshal your thoughts, and you act foolishly. When positive outcomes are visualized instead of negative ones, you prepare your thoughts for success.

Some people believe that our thoughts influence the outcome because of the energy of our thoughts. They believe that energy is magnetic and that it attracts energy of similar vibration. Positive thoughts will attract positive events. Shakti Gawain, author of *Creative Visualization*, writes, "We always attract into our lives whatever we think about most, believe in most strongly, expect on the deepest levels, and/or imagine most vividly." In *Quantum Fitness*, visualization is used as a major means of achieving fitness goals. The authors write, "Visualization is not reserved for athletes only. Sales executives, pilots, dancers, musicians, actors, parents, hostesses, chefs, engineers, lovers, and students do it every day." In *Prospering Women*, Ruth Ross writes, "We first create in mental form everything we desire to produce in physical form." She gives many examples of women who used visualization to achieve career goals.

What is in the picture of the winning interview? First, there is you, alert but not nervous. You walk in and shake hands. You sit comfortably facing the interviewer directly. You look self-confident because you know what a good choice you are for the job. You feel open to the new experience of the interview and the job. Then, there is the interviewer smiling at you. Picture a smooth flow of conversation in which you give all the right answers and in which you have a chance to tell the interviewer all your best qualities. The interviewer understands and accepts what you are saying. You are really making a good impression. You are communicating in an honest and harmonious way. You are being offered the job. You feel confident and have every expectation of being interested, challenged, effective, and successful in the work. You can visualize yourself working increasingly well and being rewarded appropriately. Your visualization is exciting, optimistic, and satisfying, as well as promising of a fulfilling future.

Visualization Exercise 1

To carry out effective visualization, you need to be relaxed. You can use one of the relaxation exercises described in the first section of this chapter, or you can relax in the following way. Sit comfortably with your back straight, either cross-legged or on a chair. Close your eyes. Breathe deeply, counting backward from 10. Imagine there is a long cord going from the base of your spine way down into the earth, like the roots of a tree. Picture the energy of the earth flowing up through your spine and out the top of your head. Concentrate on this for a few minutes. Now picture the energy of the cosmos flowing into your head, through your body, and out through your feet. Try to concentrate on both these flows. Now picture yourself in the winning interview. Don't try to plan the actual words, but do try to see yourself as fully as possible. You can use the description of the winning interview above or make one up yourself. The more details about your clothes and the room that you can put in the better. Finish by saying, "This or something better now manifests itself for me in totally satisfying ways for the highest good of all concerned."

In addition to meditating about this picture, you can help create the picture in your mind in other ways. In the space below or on a separate piece of paper, you may want to draw yourself in the interview situation, or already at work in the job you want. You might also create the image by pasting up pictures of items you have cut out. Artistic ability does not count!

Visualization Exercise 2

This exercise is based on your personal affirmations. Affirmations are firm, positive statements that say that what you want is already so. Develop a list of affirmations that reflect your goals for a winning interview. Some affirmations you might have on your list would be:

"I am the best person for the job."

"People like me."

"I make a very good impression in the interview."

"I get along with new people easily."

"The interviewer thinks I am the best candidate for the job."

"I have been offered the job at _____."

"I have a very satisfying, well-paying job."

"The job I have is satisfying in every way."

Make up your own list of affirmations. Write them down. Say them several times a day. Use one of the relaxation methods and say your affirmations just as you finish relaxing. Always end by saying, "This or something better now manifests itself for me in totally satisfying ways for the highest good of all concerned."

_____

_____

_____

_____

_____

_____

_____

_____

_____

_____

_____

The visualization exercises were adapted from *Creative Visualization.* You can use other methods that you may have read about to use your energy, turning it from fear to power. The important thing is to concentrate on your goals and to picture yourself achieving them.

Rational Thinking

This section of the chapter deals with reducing nervousness through changing your thinking. It is based on the ideas of Rational-Emotive Therapy as defined by Albert Ellis and others. It is a technique that has been adapted for many self-help books, including the bestseller *Your Erroneous Zones* by Wayne Dyer.

The first thing to recognize is that you hold irrational ideas. In fact, we all do. These are ideas that we seem to have as far back as we can remember. No one knows whether we were born holding these ideas or whether we got them from people around us. The important thing is that irrational thinking keeps us from moving ahead and makes us nervous about situations.

Thoughts are irrational when they are too general to be true or useful, yet we all repeat them often. In this case, words can harm us because they reinforce a negative and irrational way of looking at life instead of allowing us to move forward and do something about life. Here are some typical irrational thoughts that most people have at various times.

"I can't stand it."

"It would be awful."

"I'm worthless."

"He, she, or it made me do it."

"Things should be different."

If you are having irrational thoughts about upcoming job interviews, a nightmare paragraph something like this one is probably going through your mind over and over:

"I'll never get a job. Interviewers are out to get you. They'll make me make mistakes. I'm such a fool. I really can't do anything right. It isn't fair that I have to go for this interview. Things should be different. If I don't do well at this job, it will be awful. I can't stand it."

Notice how easily the generally used irrational thoughts can be applied to the interview situation!

If none of the irrational thoughts in the list above go through your mind, and if the paragraph of thoughts seems completely foreign to you, then you can skip the rest of this section. If you are having irrational thoughts, however, these are affecting your emotions and contributing to the nervousness you feel. The rest of this section will deal with counteracting the thoughts.

The most important tools for counteracting irrational thoughts are a notebook and a pen or pencil. You need to set aside time to examine the thoughts and see how well the facts of life and logic support them. Doing this on a regular basis will help you in times of crisis, like going for a job interview.

The following is a worksheet to begin your rational thinking interview notebook.

Rational Thinking Worksheet

I'll burst into coughing / sneezing fit   *I've taken flu remedy. I'll explain at start of interview that I've been ill.*

Use the worksheet below to counteract your irrational thoughts about job interviews, or use it to begin a notebook to help you use rational thinking not only in interview preparation, but in many areas of your life.

I'll run over time on presentation   *I'll make sure in advance that I have method of watching the clock.*

Irrational Thought	Fact
Sample: Interviewers will make me make mistakes.	Sample: No one can control my mind. Sometimes I make mistakes. Everyone does.
1. *Some one else earmarked for the job*	*Nonsense. They only want the best candidate*
2. *I won't remember everything. I don't know enough.*	*Nonsense. I've eight years experience. I know about everything in the SW.*
3. *I won't be able to structure my thoughts*	*I can take my time + think through responses.*
4. *I'll be too nervous to listen.*	*I can take my time to listen + to remember key phrases in my answer*
5. *I'm a bit girly*	*People say I'm dynamic, possess poise + charisma. I look good + powerful.*
6. *I'll drop all the papers.*	*I'll just take my time to get settled.*
7. *I can't control my nerves*	*I can evoke feelings of calm. This is no worse than presents to all MDs at Essec etc*

Summary Worksheet

In this chapter, you saw three ways to conquer nervous energy and convert it to positive use. One way is to practice relaxation. A second way is to use visualization techniques and affirmations. A third way is to challenge irrational thoughts through an examination of facts and the use of logic. You can use any one or any combination of the techniques that seems best for you. However, each of them works best if practiced all the time, not just when critical situations like job interviews occur.

Use the checklist below to review your options to nervousness.

_____ I have thought about ways to convert nervous energy to creative or productive energy. I can:

_____

_____

_____

_____

_____ I have chosen the method or methods that seem right for me. They are:

_____

_____

_____

_____

_____ I practice these methods regularly. My schedule is:

_____

_____

_____

_____

Twelve Key Steps to a Winning Interview

In this chapter you concentrated on

Key Step 8: Turn nervous energy into positive energy through relaxation, visualization, and rational thinking.

DURING THE INTERVIEW

Section II

What to Expect

If you are about to go for your very first job interview, you are probably wondering what to expect. Who will interview me? How many people will be there? What kinds of questions will they ask? Even if you have gone for several job interviews, you may not know how typical they were. Will all the interviews I go to be the same? This chapter will help you recognize some interview types, become familiar with often-used formats, and see the questions you can expect to be asked.

Most of the people who will interview you have no training in how to conduct a personnel interview. Most of the people who will interview you spend little of their total working time interviewing prospective employees. Why is this so? Why is this important?

Large organizations often have personnel departments with trained interviewers. However, in smaller companies, people do many jobs. Someone who is a manager or the owner of the company may be an expert in managing or in the product or service of the organization, but he or she is *not* trained in personnel work. Even in a large company, after you are screened by the personnel department interviewer, if you succeed in that interview, you will probably be interviewed by the person in charge of the department and by another person with technical knowledge of your work.

Many people were interviewed for this book. Among them were the vice-president of a bank, the principal of a large high school, the manager of an advertising company, a partner in an accounting company, a senior analyst in a software design house, and a fashion designer in a large corporation. Each of them had participated extensively in hiring. Only one of them had received any training, and he estimated that he had hired professionals for more than 100 positions before he underwent the training.

This is an important fact to remember in reading this chapter. Typical patterns for interviews can be explained, and the questions usually asked can be listed, but the people interviewing you may never have read a textbook on interviewing. They will do things their own ways. However, it was interesting to see that the employers interviewed did end up being more similar to each other in their approaches than different.

> **Key Step 9:** Know the types of interviews and their general format.

Types of Interviews

There are two ways of looking at the different types of interviews. One way is to look at how many people will be present during the interview itself. The second way is to examine the level of structure of the questions.

It is very rare for a person to be hired on the basis of one interview with one person, unless the company or organization hiring is very small. When we asked the successful employees how many interviews they had had for their current job, the lowest number was two, and the highest was eight. Many of the interviews had been with two people. All of the employers also reported that their organizations conducted at least two interviews before hiring a successful candidate.

Sequential interviews are used most often. In this method, the candidate passes from one interview to the next if he or she is successful at the early one. Often the first interview is a screening interview with one or more members of the personnel department. Later interviews are with managers and with people familiar with the demands of the job such as the immediate supervisor. You would be interviewed by one or at most two people at a time.

Serial interviews seem the same as sequential interviews to the applicants because they see one interviewer after another. The difference is that no decision is made until after all the interviews take place.

Panel interviews enable several people to interview the candidate at one time. These usually take place in large organizations, particularly in filling middle management and higher government jobs. The panel is usually made up of someone from the personnel department, someone from the management of the organization, and someone with a knowledge of the needs and demands of the job. Sometimes members of the general public with an identifiable interest in the selection process will be included. For example, one of the employees was interviewed for a job as a high school principal. The panel consisted of the assistant superintendent of the district, teachers from several departments, a school secretary, and a parent.

Sometimes interviewers have all their questions prepared ahead of time. All of the candidates are then rated on their responses to the same questions. This kind of highly *structured interview* is used most often in panel interviews and interviews by the personnel department. The opposite of this is the *unstructured interview*. In this kind of interview, all of the questions flow from the interchange between the interviewer and the applicant. Practically speaking, most interviews fall somewhere in between the two. The employer starts with particular questions to ask. Other questions come as a result of what you have said or what the employer sees on your resume or application.

A particular type of interview that is sometimes used is the *problem-solving interview*. In this, the candidates are given one or several practical problems and asked how they would solve them. For example, a problem with a fellow employee who does not do her or his share of the work load will be described. The candidates will be asked how they would handle this situation. Specific answers from the candidate then trigger other questions from the interviewer. This technique is often used in panel interviews.

The Interview Format
In *Management's Guide to Effective Employment Interviewing*, Roland T. Ramsey gives four elements of the successful interview, from the employer's point of view. The four steps are:

1. Prepare and review.
2. Establish rapport.
3. Exchange information.
4. Close the interview.

These steps seem to come naturally because all of the employers interviewed described using something similar. A closer look at each of the four steps follows.

Interviewers prepare. You can expect that interviewers have read your resume, application, and any other information they have about you. (That does not mean they have memorized your resume.) They have also thought about the job for which you are being interviewed. They know, to some extent, the kind of person they want and the kind of skills that person should have. They probably have also formulated, either deliberately or through habit, some questions they know they are going to ask.

Interviewers try to establish rapport, that is, they try to establish a comfortable relationship with you so that you are both speaking the same language. Some of the employers said they try to establish rapport by making small talk, asking a question like, "Did you get here O.K.?" Most of them ask some general questions about your interest in the job. Opening questions the surveyed employers gave us included:

"I see your last job was at the ABC Company. Tell me something about what you did there."

"Why don't you tell me about your background and what you're looking for, and I'll tell you about the firm. Then we'll take it from there."

"Why do you want to be a computer consultant?"

"I understand you're interested in going into teaching."

Even the most formal panel interviews often begin with a question like, "Tell us something about your background and what you have been doing up to this point." (In the next chapter, you will see how to answer these opening questions and others.)

Exchanging information is, of course, the heart of the interview. If you look back at the employers' goals in the first chapter, you will see the kind of knowledge they are trying to gain. You have information about yourself you want to communicate, and you have also identified information about the job and organization which you want to gain. You have already begun to prepare for the exchange of information by examining your goals and by preparing an assessment of your strengths in chapter 3.

The interview closing can be handled in several different ways. Often you will be asked if there is anything more you want to say about yourself, or if you have any questions. When employers were asked for typical or standard last questions, they said:

> "How does all this sound to you? Is this the job you thought you were applying for?"

> "Do you have any more questions about our firm?"

> "Is there anything you would like to say or add?"

> "I close by talking about the company and giving the applicant some brochures."

All of the employers said they give the applicant some idea of the next step.

"We'll be in touch with you in a week or two."

"Thank you for coming by. I don't think your qualifications fit this job exactly. I will call you if we have an opening more suited to your skills."

"We are interviewing a number of highly qualified applicants for this job. That process should be finished in two weeks, and you will be hearing from us shortly after that."

> **Key Step 10:** Know the kinds of questions you will probably be asked.

The Questions   There are many lists of questions that can be drawn up as samples of what to expect in an interview. However, it is important to remember in looking at the questions that the interviewer is trying to see more about you than the answer to any one question can reveal. Remember the phrases that employers used to describe the qualities they look for in a prospective employee:

- capability
- potential
- genuine interest in the job
- genuine interest in the firm
- appropriate background
- expertise
- relevant interests
- ability to relate to others
- ability to deal with authority
- independent decision-making skills
- ability to fit in socially
- ability to fit in technically

You can expect questions not just about the facts of your education, job experience, and interests, but about your attitudes and feelings toward them. The interviewers will probably ask some questions about how you feel about their company. They may ask questions about your future plans to try to assess your commitment to their job or company. You may also expect to have some questions that show you know your work and are up-to-date in the field. These are the hardest questions to find in any textbook or to put on a list because they are different for every job.

The list of questions that follows comes from a variety of books for management about interviewing and from the responses of both employers and employees in our surveys. Look at the list to see how varied questions about the same thing can be. See how specific some are and how general others are. Use this list to prepare for interviews by thinking through answers that show your strengths.

Question List 1—Education

What were your major courses of study in school?

_____

_____

Why did you choose those courses?

_____

_____

What was the most important thing you learned in school?

_____

_____

Why did you decide to go to University X?

_____

_____

Do you plan to finish your college degree while you are working?

_____

_____

Did school meet your expectations or were you disappointed?

_____

_____

How did you pay for your college education?

_____

_____

To what extent do your grades reflect how much you learned?

_____

_____

Do you feel your education was worthwhile?

_____

_____

Question List 2—Work Experience

What were your major responsibilities at your last job?

_____

_____

At the job before that?

_____

_____

Which of your previous jobs did you like (or dislike) most? Why?

_____

_____

What was the most rewarding experience at work?

_____

_____

What do you find most satisfying in a job?

_____

_____

What was your single most important accomplishment for the company in your last job?

_____

_____

Why did you leave Company X?

_____

_____

Why do you want to change jobs?

_____

_____

What was the toughest problem you had to solve?

_____

_____

How did you solve it?

_____

_____

Question List 3—The New Job and the Future

Why do you want to work for this company?

_____

This job means you will have to relocate; what problems do you see for your family?

_____

This job has a lot of travel; how will you handle that?

_____

After a description of the job: How do you see yourself fitting in with this job?

_____

What skills did you learn on your last job that you can use here?

_____

Why do you want to do what we do in this company?

_____

How do you think your education will help you on this job?

_____

Where do you want to be five (ten) years from now?

_____

What would you do if you were fired in two years?

_____

What kinds of additional education, formal or informal, do you think you need to meet your career goals?

_____

If you went to work for us today, what job would you like to hold in three to five years?

_____

How long do you plan on staying with us?

_____

Summary Worksheet

This chapter gave you a preview of what to expect in an interview. You saw that interviews can be conducted by one, two, or many people. They can range from the highly structured, with all questions prepared beforehand, to the very informal. Lists of questions about your education, job experience, the new job, and the future helped you think about what you will talk about during the interview.

In the *Employer's Guide to Hiring and Firing*, Paul Preston gives employers a "Summary of the Interview Do's." It is also an excellent summary for the candidate. Expect to be asked the following. Ask yourself, can I answer questions about:

_____ More detailed information on the items on my application form or resume

_____ My reasons for leaving former jobs

_____ The kinds of references I will receive

_____ Profiles of my past job activities and responsibilities

_____ Likes and dislikes about my past jobs

_____ My preferences and desires in the job I am seeking—duties, hours, wages, working conditions

_____ My self-evaluation of strengths and weaknesses for this job and others in the company

---

Twelve Key Steps to a Winning Interview

In this chapter you concentrated on

Key Step 9: Know the types of interviews and their general format.   and

Key Step 10: Know the kinds of questions you will probably be asked.

Giving Winning Answers

The heart of the interview is the give and take in which, for the most part, the interviewer asks questions, and you answer them. No one can tell you what answers to give since these must come from your own experiences. However, you can learn how to deliver the information in your answers so that you are most effective in creating a favorable impression on the employer.

Listening

Listening is the key to winning answers and to a winning interview.

You saw that the first objective of the interviewer is to establish rapport, a sense that the two of you are communicating in a way you both understand, that you are "speaking the same language," "operating on the same wavelength."

The earlier this sense of communication is established in the interview, the better the interview will be because the interviewer will come away with a fuller sense of you as a person. Obviously this sense of being on the same wavelength has to happen for both of you. You can help this along by listening carefully to the interviewer. In the book *The Seven Habits of Highly Effective People*, careful listening is identified as a critical habit. Habit Five is "seek first to understand, then to be understood."

You let someone know you are listening to them by facing them and by maintaining eye contact. Studies of human behavior, particularly of Americans, show that people look directly at someone when they are listening even more than when they are speaking. You want to appear comfortable and relaxed in the interview. How will you handle this? First, be sure to sit facing the interviewer directly; second, look at the interviewer's face, focusing primarily on the eyes. You communicate that you are listening.

One of the most important reasons for listening to the interviewer is so that you can hear the question. People who don't listen, who are jumping ahead in their minds to answer questions they have not heard, do not do well in interviews. Not only do they fail to provide the information requested, but they come across as poor communicators, as being "out of it." The question, "Tell me something about your last job" is very different from the question, "What were your major responsibilities on your last job?" The first question allows you to deal with whatever aspect of the job you thought was important and to relate that to the job you are being interviewed for. The second question calls for a direct, more factual response.

A major part of listening is not interrupting. Sometimes it is hard to tell if interviewers have finished speaking or are just pausing to gather thoughts or breathe. Generally speaking, you can tell from watching them. If they turn to you, or look at you, they probably want a response. On the other hand, if they are looking into the distance or down at their desk, they are probably just pausing in their speech.

Remember, many interviewers are not trained. Even though it's your interview, they may spend a lot more time talking than you do. One employee told a story of going for an interview which began, "Let me tell you something about the job and this company." Ten minutes later, the interviewer was just finishing an elaborate explanation complete with a table of organization and company brochures. It was important for the applicant to pay attention throughout that recital, storing away information to be used in her own answers.

> **Key Step 11:** Be prepared to answer a wide variety of questions.

Answering—the Specific and the General

Some parts of the interview will deal with specific questions about your background and experiences. Reviewing samples of these questions in the last chapter, looking over your own resume, and analyzing your strengths and experiences in chapter 3 will help you prepare for these questions. Answer a specific question with specific detail that shows you at your best.

Covey, the author of *The Seven Habits of Highly Effective People*, describes a key model for interview success that he calls "solution selling." He describes counseling people who want better jobs "to study the industry, even the specific problems the organizations they are interested in are facing, and then to develop an effective presentation showing how their abilities can help solve the organization's problems."

If the interviewer asks "What was your most important course in college?" Do not answer, "Lunch." Do not answer "Gym," unless you are applying for a job in recreation. Answer with the name of a course or several courses related to the field you are in, and explain why this course was important to you then and now. Here is a good answer:

"The most important course I took was Behavioral Decision Making. It gave me an extensive knowledge of the theory and research in group and organizational influence on how people make decisions. I have found this very important in helping me understand how decisions are made in the company for which I work now. The course was practical too because I can see the kinds of things that I might do if I were a leader trying to bring about change in my group."

General or vague questions are harder to answer. Interviewers often use general questions to see what you will choose to say. When asked a general question, you have to make a series of quick choices. First, you have to decide whether to answer the question, or whether to ask a question about it. The interviewer may say, for example, "Tell me about your background." You can ask, "Would you like me to start with my education or my work experience?" On the other hand, you can use that opportunity to point up your strengths, knowledge of the job, and information about the company. As soon as you have made the choice to answer the question, you have to decide where in your background to begin. As often as possible, try to use general questions to give the information you decided you wanted to communicate in your analysis of strengths. Of course, if a question is really vague and you have no idea what the interviewer means, ask for clarification.

It is very rare not to have at least one general question about your background. It may take the form of something like, "Tell me about yourself," or "Tell me why you think you should get this job," or any one of hundreds of other phrasings. Often an interview begins and ends with this kind of general question. Be prepared. Don't memorize an answer because you cannot be sure of the exact form the question will take. Do use the worksheets in chapter 3 to get ready.

Sometimes an interviewer will ask a vague question out of ignorance or misinformation. This happened to one of the successful applicants we interviewed. "It was a panel interview, and the interviewer's follow-up question was inappropriate because his facts were wrong. Basically, I tried to save his face by giving a good answer slightly changing his facts." She got the job!

Answering Problem-Solving Questions

Often in the course of an interview, you will be asked to solve a hypothetical problem. You will be given a situation and asked how you would act. A panel interview may consist of one problem-solving question after another, but any type of interview will probably have at least one.

The first thing to do is think. Don't be afraid to take some time to plan your answer. The interviewer will respect you more. Try to hear the entire problem when it is first presented, but if it is complicated and you have missed some part, ask for clarification.

Answer as if you were already in the job. This is particularly important if the job you are moving into is a higher supervisory role. Do not answer as a secretary if you are applying for a job as office manager.

Remember that you are part of an organization. One of the key questions in the interviewer's mind is: "Do I want this person on my team?" While you do not want to go running to your boss too quickly, you also do not want to seem to be taking on the whole world by yourself. Think of the resources and operating procedure of the organization that you would use in solving the problem.

If all or part of your approach is challenged, stick to your point as long as it makes sense to you. You want to appear to be decisive but not inflexible. If the interviewer consistently pushes you in some direction you did not take, listen and think. If you can see the interviewer's point of view, accept it with some further explanation of when you would switch to that approach. If the interviewer's direction continues to seem wrong, don't change your first answer, elaborate on it.

Responding to Stress Questions

None of the employers interviewed for this book try to introduce stress into the interview situation. On the contrary, they all expressed a desire to make the candidate as comfortable as possible. However, textbooks on interviewing do describe two kinds of stress-producing techniques that interviewers may use.

The first kind of stress interview is the rapid-fire series of questions. This is used in some jobs where you can expect to meet stress on the job. Follow the same steps as for all questions. Listen, think, answer. Do not let yourself be pressured into giving answers you know are wrong. Do not lose your temper. Try to keep looking at the interviewer. Try not to fidget with your hair or your clothes.

The second kind of stress interview employs silence. After you finish speaking, the interviewer says nothing. Of course, the interviewer may just be inexperienced and not have anything to say. Resist the temptation to fill the gap. It is the interviewer's job to keep the interview moving. Do not repeat or elaborate on your answer. Do not mumble under your breath. Do not imagine that you have suddenly gone bald or there is a fly on your nose. This will lead you to move about appearing fidgety. Just wait.

Generally speaking, most employers feel there is enough stress in an interview without the need for introducing any artificially.

Dealing with a Weakness

Very few of us are perfect. You may have a weakness that comes from some gap in your education or experience—a weakness from something you did not do; or you may have a weakness such as having been fired from a job—a weakness from something you did.

You must recognize and understand your own weaknesses. If you do not, when one of them is brought up in an interview, you will be unprepared and tend to make it worse than it is.

The employers interviewed were not in agreement as to whether you should bring up the weakness or let it emerge in the interview. They were in agreement that you should understand your weaknesses and have productive explanations. In *The Interviewer's Manual*, which is primarily for employers, there is some advice for job candidates. If you identify weaknesses, think of remedial steps you can take such as further schooling or training.

If your weakness is from something you did not do, try to turn it into a strength or show how you have compensating strengths. One of the employers said the best credential is an answer like, "I don't know how to do X, but when I was in my previous job, I didn't know how to do Y. Then I read such and such a book, and I was able to do it." This answer demonstrates the ability to learn. Another employer said, "If you quit college and bummed around Europe for two years, don't say that and don't bring it up. But if you learned languages while you were in Europe, that's important. Bring it up."

The same employer said, "The biggest problem a candidate can create is to be deceitful or appear to be deceitful." The need for honesty is mentioned in this section on weaknesses because it is here that one might be most tempted to lie. There is a big difference between dishonesty and discretion. Discretion means that you do not have to reveal all your thoughts about yourself or anyone else. You do not have to say that you left a job "because it was boring, boring, boring!" Better to say that you left it for a more challenging job. You cannot, however, say that you graduated from college if you did not. The first is a good use of discretion. The second is dishonest.

Other weaknesses in your background come from what you have done, in particular, leaving a former job under less than the best circumstances—being fired. In dealing with these weaknesses, it is very important that you do not appear hypercritical of your previous company and that you do not attack your former boss. One of the employers interviewed said, "I know all the companies in my field and what their weaknesses are. Rather than emphasizing negative things, the candidate should just say, 'The job didn't work out.' " Another employer said, "One of the worst things a person can do is be very judgmental about the company they worked for. If they think they know everything about running that company, that's probably what they will think of our company. They should say something like, 'I didn't get along with the manager of my department, but I can think of some things I might have done differently.' They shouldn't say, 'No one could get along with that manager. He had no idea of what he was doing.' "

The basic way of dealing with weakness, then, is to be honest but discreet, to show you take responsibility for your own actions, and to show you know how to build on your strengths.

Answering Inappropriate Questions—Know Your Rights

There are a number of areas about which an employer may not ask questions. These areas have been defined by the United States Constitution, federal laws and regulations, state laws, and court decisions. The purpose of the laws and decisions is to prevent discrimination in hiring on the basis of age; sex; racial, religious, or ethnic background; or handicapping conditions.

It is important that you be aware of the areas that are inappropriate and illegal and that you consider what you will do if you are asked a question in any of these areas. While it is illegal for the employer to ask for the information, it is not illegal for you to supply it. So you have some choice should one of these areas come up.

Questions about your race, religion, or ethnic origin cannot be asked. This includes questions like:

"Where does your family come from?"

"That's an interesting last name. What nationality is it?"

"What's your native language?" (You can be asked about fluency in languages other than English if that is applicable to the duties of the job.)

Questions about your age are not permitted. This includes questions like:

"How old are you?"

"I see you graduated from college in 19____. How old were you then?"

Questions about marital status or children are not legal. This includes questions like:

"Are you married?"

"What kind of work does your husband (or wife) do?"

"Do you plan to be married?"

"Do you plan to have any children?"

"How old are your children?"

Questions about height, weight, health, or handicapping conditions that are not related to the requirements of a job are also illegal.

There are also questions that are inappropriate such as questions about your personal life, whom you live with, whom you date, and who your friends are.

If you feel you have been asked an illegal or inappropriate question, you can refuse to answer the question saying something like, "I really feel that information is not related to the job, and I do not want to discuss it." You might say, "I think that question is not allowed under the equal opportunity laws. I am not going to answer it." You can decide to give a brief answer and then say, "I think there are more important and relevant things about me in relationship to this job. I would rather talk about them."

Since it is not illegal for you to answer the question, you have to assess the situation. How do you feel about answering the question? How do you feel about your potential employer if he or she is asking this kind of question? Sometimes you may feel that the person asking the question is just making conversation. However, so much has been written about the equal opportunity laws that it is hard to believe that someone interviewing is not aware of the law. If your answer will not hurt you, you can choose to answer the question.

If you refuse to answer the question, that may mean you will not get the job. This in itself is discrimination. Of course, answering the question does not ensure your getting the job.

If you believe you have been discriminated against on an illegal basis, you do have steps you can take. You can file a complaint with the Equal Employment Opportunity Commission in Washington, D.C. You can also contact the Fair Employment Practices Commission of your state to see what information they prohibit in employment selection interviews. Based on this, you can file a complaint in your state. You may also sue the company using your own attorney.

Do not go into an interview expecting to be asked illegal

questions. Most employers are familiar with the laws and abide by them, at least in applications and interviews. Beginning with suspicions that you will face illegal questions will divert you from your true purpose, to be offered the job you want.

Avoid These—A List of Do Not's

Do not use jargon and abbreviations. Most companies have their own vocabulary made up of company words and abbreviations. Avoid using these in an interview. Don't talk about OTPS, and PO's. Talk about a budget for supplies and services and purchase orders.

Do not use jokes to answer questions. One employer remembered a candidate who was in front of a panel interview. The candidate was asked, "What do you expect from your secretary?" The candidate said, "Tender loving care!" The secretary was on the panel, and the candidate did not get the job.

Do not be negative about your previous or present job or company. That company and job will go on without you. Negativity creates the impression that you do not take responsibility for what you do. It also makes the interviewer side with your previous company and worry about your ability to get along in general.

Do not know it all. One of the employers said the worst thing is when a candidate says, "They didn't know how to run their business. I could really have improved things for them." This creates the impression that you will be judgmental about any company and will not be a good team player.

Do not allow wrong impressions to remain. If the interviewer has really misunderstood something you have said, or has incorrect facts about you, politely correct him. Say, "I believe I was not completely clear when I explained my last job. Although I did some selling, I was the sales manager, not one of the salespeople."

Do not memorize answers. Interviewers expect you to be spontaneous, not perfect. A memorized answer makes it seem like interviewing is your job, rather than interviewing being a means to get a job.

Do not go to the interview unprepared. You need to review your strengths, your weaknesses, the demands of the job, and all you can about the organization to have a winning interview.

Summary Worksheet

This chapter included tips on answering questions. Review the major points below before going to an interview.

_____ I listen to the interviewer.

_____ I understand the difference between specific and general questions.

_____ I know how to use general questions to provide information I want the interviewer to have about me.

_____ I ask for clarification if I need it.

_____ I think before answering problem-solving questions.

_____ I am prepared to deal with silence and other stress-provoking situations.

_____ I know my weaknesses and can deal with them honestly but discreetly.

_____ I know my rights in the interview, but I don't expect them to be challenged.

_____ I am careful to avoid jargon, inappropriate humor, quick judgments, and hypercritical answers.

_____ I correct wrong impressions.

_____ I prepared, but did not memorize answers.

Twelve Key Steps to a Winning Interview

In this chapter you concentrated on

Key Step 11: Be prepared to answer a wide variety of questions.

Asking Winning Questions

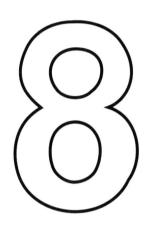

In the very first chapter of this book, you identified your needs in a job and translated these into information goals. You thought through the kind of organization for which you would like to work, the working conditions you want, the salary and benefits you are seeking, and the career goals you are pursuing. This chapter is about how to get the information you want during the interview process, and how to do that in a way that improves your chances of having a winning interview.

The key to using questions for a winning interview is knowing *when* to ask the questions. We asked the employers we interviewed what questions they found appropriate, and which ones they found inappropriate. Here are some of their answers:

> "I like when people ask about the size of our organization and their opportunity for advance-

ment in it. I like them to ask about their duties and the kinds of clients they'll be dealing with. Of course, they need to know about benefits and vacation too."

"I like a candidate to ask questions that show he has done his research. For example, 'What age group will I be dealing with?' 'What kind of students will I be teaching?' I like task-related questions."

"I don't like questions which imply a person will be watching the clock and leaving at the first possible minute—'How much money will I make?' 'What are the hours?' "

"I don't like questions which reveal the person will do the minimum amount of work—when she wants to know her rights right away."

"It's okay if people don't have any questions. The best questions are about the structure of the company, its business, the immediate supervisor."

"Inappropriate questions show an over-interest in vacation and benefits—'How many sick days are there in a year?' "

"It's good when someone asks about the potential for advancement and shows an interest in using his abilities—'I've also done such and such, do you have any use for it?' "

"I like to see that someone is interested in promotion, but not in time limits. I don't want someone too restless."

"The worst thing someone can ask about is hours—'Is there much homework?' As far as the company is concerned, they can't put in too many hours. If it means they have to work on a weekend, let them work. Any question about work load is the end for that applicant."

An analysis of the employer's feelings about questions is consistent with everything else they have said. They want someone who is strongly interested in doing the job for their organization. They want you if you want the job, not just its benefits. Of course, work is an economic activity. Everyone knows that salary and benefits are important, but the most important thing, the employers are saying, is the work itself, the job of the job. This means you have to ask the right questions at the right time.

> **Key Step 12:** Know the questions you want answered and when to ask them.

Questions about Salary

Do not ask about salary or benefits until you are offered a job or the interviewer brings it up. Although this information may be of vital interest to you, remember to picture the interview from the employer's point of view. You are selling your services to the employer. The employer has not decided whether or not to buy them. If you were selling a valuable object, you would not begin with its price tag!

Once you have been offered a job, you can ask what the salary or salary range of the job is. At that time, you may also ask about any of the benefits that are important to you and appropriate to the job. If none of the benefits will make a difference in whether or not you accept a job, it is best that you do not ask about them until after you are hired, since salary and benefits are often a matter of overall negotiation. There may be benefits that are important to you but will not make the difference between your accepting and rejecting a job offer. Look at the questions about salary and benefits in the worksheet that follows. Put a star next to the ones you will want to discuss before accepting a job. Put a check next to the ones you will ask after accepting employment. You will also see space for some questions of your own.

Salary and Benefits Question Worksheet

_____ 1. What is my starting salary?

_____ 2. How are salary increases determined?

_____ 3. What kind of health insurance plan can I get?

_____ 4. Who pays for the health insurance?

_____ 5. Is there a dental benefits plan?

_____ 6. Is there any reimbursement for college or graduate school expense?

_____ 7. How will I be reimbursed for work-related travel expenses?

_____ 8. Does this position qualify for stock options?

_____ 9. Does this position include a company car?

_____ 10. How much does the company pay for relocation expenses?

_____ 11. What is my total compensation package?

_____ 12. How many vacation days do I get a year?

_____ 13. What restrictions are there, if any, on taking vacation?

_____ 14. What is the organization's sick leave policy?

_____ 15. What hours will I work?

_____ 16. Is there overtime pay or compensatory time off?

Notes of additional benefits which might be important factors to you:

_____ 17. _____

_____ 18. _____

_____ 19. _____

_____ 20. _____

The employer may bring up the salary earlier in the interview process. There are generally three ways in which the employer can ask you about salary. You need to be prepared to answer each of these questions:

1. "What salary are you willing to accept?" If you are an experienced worker, you probably know the answer to this question, based on your previous jobs. If you are just starting out, it is important that you do your research and have some idea of the salaries being offered in your field. Giving a realistic response shows your knowledge.

2. "What is your current salary?" Your answer to this question can vary with your goals. If you feel your current salary is in line with the industry wage for your job, you can give an exact figure, "$43,000." If you want to be somewhat more general, you can say, "the mid-forties." If your current salary is too low, and you really will not move unless you get something considerably higher, you can answer the question that wasn't asked and say "My minimum salary requirement to move is $45,000."

3. "The salary range for this job is $42,000 to $45,000. How does that sound to you?" Your answer should indicate either that the range is acceptable or unacceptable. If you believe it is too low, you can ask how the range is determined and what the next range is. If you feel you qualify for the next range, you can then say why this is so.

Questions about the Job

During the interview, it is appropriate to ask questions about the nature of the work you will be doing if hired and about the organization itself.

One word of caution: these questions show interest only if you are really interested in the answer. Most of us are not accomplished actors. We cannot convince other people that we feel something we do not feel. If you really want the answer to a question, ask it. If not, do not!

Listed on the next worksheet are some good job-related questions. Put a star next to the ones you would like to ask in an interview. Space is also provided for your own questions.

Job Question Worksheet

_____ 1. What will be the major responsibilities of this job?

_____ 2. Where does this job fit in the overall organization?

_____ 3. In which location will I work?

_____ 4. What specific projects do you see me starting first?

_____ 5. What is a typical career path from this job in your company?

_____ 6. Why did the person previously in the job leave?

_____ 7. Who will be my immediate supervisor? Can I meet her or him?

_____ 8. Your annual reports show steady growth over the last three years. How rapidly do you plan to grow over the next three years?

_____ 9. Are there particular customers you would like me to deal with?

_____ 10. What is the nature of the population your organization serves?

Additional questions that may be of importance to you.

11. _____

_____

_____

12. _____

_____

_____

13. _____

_____

_____

14. _____

_____

_____

15. _____

_____

_____

Questions to End the Interview

When you leave any interview, it is important to know what to expect next. Sometimes in highly structured situations, you will have been notified of the entire process. Often the employer will tell you. If you do not know what the next step will be, ask the interviewer, "What will the next step in your hiring process be?" or "When may I expect to hear from you again?" Either of these questions or similar ones can be used to show interest in the job and a desire on your part to continue the process.

Fill in the following items as a reminder to yourself.

When will I talk to the interviewer again? _____

_____

Will I call or will the interviewer call me? _____

_____

What will the next step be? _____

_____

What other steps must be taken? _____

_____

_____

_____

_____

_____

_____

_____

Summary Worksheet

This chapter focused on the questions you can ask in the interview—questions about the job, the organization, about salary and benefits, and about the next step in the interview process. Review the basics below:

_____ I know my salary requirements and which benefits are important to me. They are:

_____

_____

_____

_____

_____ I understand the difference between questions about salary and questions about the job itself.

_____

_____

_____

_____

_____ I know when to ask questions about the job and when to ask questions about salary.

_____

_____

_____

_____

_____ I know how to end the interview and how to establish my continued interest in the mind of the interviewer. At the end of the interview, I will:

_____

_____

_____

_____

Twelve Key Steps to a Winning Interview

In this chapter you concentrated on

Key Step 12: Know the questions you want answered and when to ask them.

Winning the Interview

This chapter pulls together all you have learned about having a winning interview and gives you some final advice from the experts—the employers and the winning employees.

Twelve Steps to a Winning Interview

It is important to remember that an interview is not a contest between you and the employer. A winning interview means that you both end up on the same team. Listed on page 100 are the twelve key steps you have learned to take to create winning interviews.

Twelve Key Steps to a Winning Interview

1. Understand the employer's point of view.
2. Develop your own information goals.
3. Get all the interview appointment information you need.
4. Assess your own strengths and weaknesses.
5. Learn all you can about the job and organization.
6. Match your skills to the job requirements.
7. Plan how you will look as carefully as you plan what to say.
8. Turn nervous energy into positive energy through relaxation, visualization, and rational thinking.
9. Know the types of interviews and their general format.
10. Know the kinds of questions you will probably be asked.
11. Be prepared to answer a wide variety of questions.
12. Know the questions you want answered and when to ask them.

Knowing the twelve steps and putting them all together is what makes a winning interview. That is what creates the overall impression that makes the employer want to hire you. The two sections that make up the rest of this chapter give you winning tips from the employers and winning tips from the employees who succeeded.

Winning Tips from Employers
Start off right

Employers emphasize the importance of the applicant's opening remarks, the communication of sincerity, and the idea that applicants must not allow themselves to be discouraged by rejection, or by the feeling of how little control they have over the situation.

"I want the person to walk in and be ready to shake my hand. I want them to expect to be shown where to sit. A lot of headhunters say that the interviewee should take over the interview. I don't think so. They have to let it happen to them."

Give winning answers

"People have to be really able to describe their skills and what they have done. On any project, one or two do all the work. The others are passengers on the ride. We don't want any passengers."

"There are certain things: an animation in the face, an expressiveness that's obviously appropriate, the ability to give an extended reply, the ability to present ideas in a logical fashion, not jumping all over the place."

"It's no good if a person gives one or two word answers, and I have the burden of extracting information. People should also speak loud enough in relation to the distance from me, in a conversational tone, so that I don't have to keep asking them to repeat what they said."

"In some of our jobs, the person has to work with clients; in others, they just sit in a cubicle by themselves. Of course, I expect more social skills from the first."

"There is a lot of pressure to come to the interview ready to take charge. Let the burden be on the interviewer. Seize opportunities to present your strengths, but let silences and awkward moments occur."

Be honest

"I put a sense of sincerity and integrity very high—very, very high."

"If he shows things that contradict characteristics he is supposed to have, if he strikes me as a phoney, I don't want him."

Look your best

"No matter what the level of the job, the person must be clean and neat, but not super flashy or too rich looking."

"When you go for an interview you must really be on your toes. This is your audition. You should have an above average appearance, an intelligent look, even if this isn't how you look all the time."

"I don't like trendy clothes for men or women, anything that has a bohemian quality. I'm very conservative that way."

Create a lasting impression

"My best advice—the simple basics. Show up on time looking respectable. Show interest in the job, the company, the kind of work you do."

"I look for someone able to think and talk on his feet."

"Once I've ascertained that they have the skills and the background, I'm looking for people who can converse normally, comfortably, as they will have to do with a client. I'm looking for them not to blow it."

"Poor grammar, nervous mannerisms, too many gestures hurt a candidate."

"The key word is *enthusiasm*. You should seem interested in yourself and the job you're applying for. You should be motivated in life."

Take heart   "Get experience. People who have had fifteen or twenty interviews do better."

"It's a somewhat random process, and very dependent on the interviewer. In my company, you could get hired one day and not the next, depending on who saw you. Remember each interviewer has his or her own set of interests and prejudices. Don't despair!"

"Be in the right place at the right time. Don't be discouraged by rejection. Interviewing is one step in the process of getting hired. Keep the process going. If you want it to happen, sometimes you have to make it happen. It's all a matter of timing."

Winning Tips from Employees   Recently hired employees talked about what made for a successful interview and how they corrected mistakes they had made in earlier ones.

Prepare   "I got information about the company from a business index, from annual reports, and by talking to people I knew."

"I indicated that I had done a lot of research for the company. I knew what the company was doing. You can't come in cold from an ad or listing."

"I was lucky about getting information about the company because I had worked for them briefly as a temporary worker. I got to know people in a few departments who I could talk to when this job came up."

Use what you have prepared   "My answer to the first question was extremely important. I knew they were going to ask me why I thought I was qualified for the job. This is my first job as a supervisor, so I told them all the supervisory and administrative things I had done in my previous jobs and in my professional organizations."

"I related my past experience to this job. I knew they needed fast turnover of the work so I talked about my newspaper experience where I had to meet deadlines quickly."

"I tried to convince them of my specific skills for the position, convince them of how I had used my skills before."

"I work in a small industry so I tried to mention a lot of names when I talked about my past experience. That way they had a lot of people to call for references."

"Usually the interviewer will ask a few broad range questions. Take any question and turn it slightly to focus on your talents. If you do it to every question, it's overbearing and no good."

Learn from each interview

"Practice going for interviews, even for jobs you don't want. You really learn."

"In my bad interviewing, I talked too much and went beyond the question asked. Not giving the other person a chance to interrupt, being too humorous, trying to make the other person like me—those were my mistakes."

"In my early interviews I was asked my best quality and my worst. I didn't have an answer. I learned to have answers more or less prepared."

"I think one of my biggest mistakes was I tended to walk in and say, 'I'm intelligent and worth hiring.' I tried to present myself as something special. Better to show yourself as 'Joe Regular.' People who hire you probably do know more than you. Anyway they want someone who will do what they want. Otherwise you're not worth anything to them. No one wants to deal with a smart aleck."

"I learned not to be put off by rejection. At first I was. I was fearful of going on to the next one. Persevere! There's an employer out there for you. Hang in! Remember, if you don't get a particular job, it's your qualifications that aren't just right, not you."

Summary Worksheet

This chapter reviewed twelve key steps to a winning interview and presented tips from people who have gone through the interviewing process on both sides of the desk. The *Employer's Guide to Hiring and Firing* gives some suggestions to employers as keys to a successful interview. They are good for you to remember too.

_____ Know the subject (for you, that's yourself, the job, the company).

_____ Concentrate on the speaker. If the speaker is dull, concentrate harder.

_____ Have a "listening posture." Look the other person in the eye. Turn toward him.

_____ Be patient. Let the other person finish what she has to say.

_____ "Stay cool." Don't overreact emotionally to words or expressions.

_____ Stay with it. Don't get distracted.

Twelve Key Steps to a Winning Interview

You have now concentrated on all twelve steps to a winning interview.

AFTER THE INTERVIEW

Maintaining Interest 10

You have finished an interview. You breathe a sigh of relief. "Whew! Glad that's over," you say to yourself. Well, it's not over. There are three more things you need to do to ensure a winning interview. First, you need to record whom you saw and any key ideas about the job or company that came out in the interview. If you are going to get a job with this organization, there will probably be more than one interview, and you will need to remember them as you go along. Second, you need to follow up the interview to maintain contact with the company. Finally, you will want to reflect about the interview so that you can use the experience in future interviews with this organization or others. This chapter covers the first two steps, record keeping and following up. The next chapter, "Experience Is the Best Teacher," is about the final step.

Record Keeping   How grand it would be to go to one interview for one job and have it end up with the employer saying, "You're just the person we've been looking for. How would you like to start work tomorrow? You name the salary." This is, however, highly unlikely. It is, therefore, important that you keep a record of each interview.

The Interview Record will help you remember who interviewed you in each company so that you are prepared for follow-up interviews. You will also use it to remember key information that you learned in the interview. You can then use the information to continue conversations in future interviews with the same people, as well as to increase your general knowledge of the company and the job.

The Interview Record is particularly important when your job search involves interviewing with more than one company. You may think when you walk out of an interview that you could never forget what happened, but once a week or two has passed, interviews tend to blur in one's mind.

An example of the Interview Record is given on the next worksheet, followed by a blank record for your use. Be sure to keep all the records for interviews with one company together. Combine them with the Interview Arrangements Worksheet you prepared when you were first called by the company or agency. The Interview Arrangements Worksheet, the results of your research, and the Interview Records form your complete file on a particular organization.

Sample Interview Record

Organization: _____*Lewis, Murrow & Company*_____ Job Applied For: _____*Systems Supervisor*_____

Address: 27 Lexington Avenue, New York, NY 10010 _____

Telephone: (212) 555-4000 _____ Date: 1/23/91 _____

Interviewers/Titles: _____*Bonnie Thornton, Partner; William Freeborne, Head of software support*_____

_____*section; Michael Pearlman, not sure.*_____

Organization Information: _____*Main focus of company shifting to include more training for clients*_____

_____*in software provided.*_____

Job Information: _____*Will include supervision of programming "interns" from local college. Travel*_____

_____*to suburbs.*_____

Salary/Benefits Information: _____*Nothing yet. Car for surburbs?*_____

Next Steps: _____*Expect to hear about another interview by 2/10. Call if no word 2/14.*_____

Interview Record

Before filling in this worksheet, make additional copies. Be sure to use one for each interview.

Organization: _____ Job Applied For: _____

Address: _____

Telephone: _____ Date: _____

Interviewers/Titles: _____

_____

_____

_____

Organization Information: _____

_____

_____

_____

_____

Job Information: _____

_____

_____

_____

_____

Salary/Benefits Information: _____

_____

_____

_____

_____

Next Steps: _____

_____

_____

Following Up There are two things you can do to follow up on an interview. One is to telephone the organization; the other is to write a letter. The employer will give you clues as to whether or not you should call and when you should do so. At the end of an interview, it is the employer's responsibility to close by telling you what to expect next. Listen carefully to what is said because that is when you will be given the clues you need.

Often the employer says, "We should be making our decision in the next few days," or words to that effect. Most of the employers surveyed said that they appreciated a call shortly after the time they mentioned had passed. They explained that they may have wanted to proceed but were busy with other matters. None of the employers said that a telephone call was harmful. Some said it would make no difference.

If the employer has given you no clues and the interview is about to end, you can use the opportunity to ask questions, to find out what the next steps in their hiring process are or when you might expect to learn their decision.

When you call, make quite clear who you are and what you are inquiring about since the employer may be involved not only in more than one hiring, but in many other aspects of business.

Example of a Follow-up Call "This is Ms. Lee. We met on January twenty-third to discuss the possibility of my coming to your company as a systems analyst. Can you tell me if any decisions have been made?"

If a secretary screens the employer's call, try to get through to the person who interviewed you. Say, "This is Mr. DeMille. I met with Ms. Harris a few days ago, and she suggested I call back now."

When you make the telephone call, you must be emotionally prepared for three kinds of answers:

1. No decision has been made yet. You can say, "I am still very interested in the job. When do you suggest I call again?"

2. A decision has been made, and you did not get the job. You can say, "I appreciate the time you spent with me. If you need someone with my qualifications in the future, I would certainly be interested in hearing from you." Of course, you would only say this if you were still interested in working for that company.

3. A decision has been made not to fill the position. This is the hardest news to hear. It feels as if you entered a contest, may have won, and the contest is cancelled just as the winner is about to be announced. You can say, "Thank you for your consideration. If the job is reopened, I would be interested in hearing from you about it."

Of course, there is always the possibility that you will call and be told, "We were just about to call you. The job is yours."

The principle behind your responses is to leave all your doors open and maintain good relationships. One of the successful employees told us that he got a job at Company B as a result of a referral from Company A where he had not been hired. Although the interviewer at Company A did not feel he had the technical qualifications needed for the specific job opening, she was impressed enough by the employee's personal qualifications to recommend him to a colleague.

A letter of thanks should be sent after every job interview. The letter should be brief and to the point. The letter reminds the employer of your existence and reinforces the impression you made.

Be sure to have all names spelled correctly and the exact titles when you write the letter. You can go back to your Interview Arrangements Worksheet, described in chapter 2, for the details. If you are missing any information, call the person who set up the interview. A sample follow-up letter appears on the next page.

Sample Follow-up Letter

P.O. Box 3892
Eugene, Oregon 97403
January 23, 199–

Ms. Gina Stewart
Information Systems Manager
Meritron Corporation
1520 Agate Street
Eugene, Oregon 97403

Dear Ms. Stewart:

  Thank you for the time you spent with me yesterday and the information about the new projects at Meritron. As you noted in our discussion, my previous experience is directly related to the responsibilities of those projects.

  I remain very interested in working at Meritron as a tax manager and look forward to speaking to you again soon.

Yours truly,

Neal J. McKinlay

Experience Is the Best Teacher

11

It may sound like a cliché, and it is. That's because it is true: experience, at least in job interviewing, *is* the best teacher. All of the successful employees interviewed stressed that they learned a great deal from their early interviews. The employers too mentioned the importance of practice.

However, experience alone is a slow teacher. You can learn even more from your interviews by actively analyzing them. Active analysis means remembering the questions you were asked and remembering your answers. It also involves a self-analysis of your answers to see what you did well and what you might have done better.

The Interview Analysis Worksheet which follows helps you look at the questions and your answers so that you can use this information in preparing for future interviews. It is best to complete a worksheet as soon as possible after an interview while events are fresh in your mind. Try to remember what happened without editing it.

Interview Analysis Worksheet

Make additional copies of this worksheet for each interview as needed.

Organization: _____

Job Applied For: _____ Date of Interview: _____

Questions I Was Asked:

1. _____

2. _____

3. _____

4. _____

5. _____

Things I Should Have Said:

1. _____

2. _____

3. _____

Things I Should *Not* Have Said:

1. _____

2. _____

3. _____

Things I Am Glad I Said:

1. _____

2. _____

3. _____

4. _____

5. _____

Be sure to review your Interview Analysis Worksheets before going for interviews in the future. Look for questions that you might be asked at many interviews, that you want to be prepared for. Look at the information you wanted to include and did not. Ask yourself how you could work in that information in response to one of the questions. Use the Interview Analysis Worksheets in conjunction with the other materials in chapter 3, "Preparing: Your Brain."

Final Summary   A last word—do not focus on the negatives. Every interview is a new experience. Focus on all the things you said and did that were good in your last interview, and build on them. Create a winning interview!

APPENDIX A: The Practice Interview—A Self-Help Exercise

The practice interview is an exercise designed to help you evaluate your interview skills. Many of the employers and employees stressed the importance of what you learn about interviewing when you go to interviews. Going through the exercise can give you preliminary or additional practice.

To do the practice interview, you will need a friend to play the part of the employer. All the directions needed for both of you are given in your separate sections: "For the Candidate" (that's you) and "For the Employer" (that's your friend).

Listed below are the steps to follow for the practice interview. They are divided into three stages—before the interview, during the interview, and after the interview.

Steps to Follow
Before the interview

1. Using the spaces provided in the section marked, "For the Candidate," prepare a job description and a description of the company.

2. Then give the job description, the company description, and a copy of your resume to the person playing the role of the employer.

3. Also give the pages marked "For the Employer" to the "employer."

4. Give the person playing the employer time to review the materials—about 10 minutes.

5. Prepare yourself for the interview using the materials provided in the "For the Candidate" section.

6. When both you and the "employer" are ready, have her or him sit at a desk or table that has an empty chair next to it.

During the interview

1. Leave the room and reenter it. THIS BEGINS THE INTERVIEW.

2. All of the directions for questioning are in the materials marked "For the Employer."

3. Go through the interview for about 20 minutes.

4. Take the practice interview seriously, and answer each question as well as you can.

After the interview

1. The "employer's" materials also contain the rating sheet. As soon as the interview is finished, the "employer" should complete the rating sheet.

2. Review the completed rating sheet. For fuller understanding, discuss the ratings with the "employer."

3. Use what you have learned to improve your performance in actual interviews.

Section I: For the Candidate

Complete the Job Description and Organization Description Worksheets below and give them to the "employer." You will also need to have a copy of your resume. Give this to the "employer" at the same time.

Job Description Worksheet

Title of Job: _____

Education Required: _____

_____

Skills Required: _____

_____

_____

_____

Major Responsibilities: _____

_____

_____

_____

Organization Description Worksheet

Name of Organization: _____

Name of Department (if any): _____

Major Product or Service of Organization: _____

_____

_____

_____

Major Product or Service of Department: _____

_____

_____

_____

Prepare for the interview

1. Review the twelve key steps to a winning interview.

2. Practice relaxation or visualization techniques.

3. Consider the salary and other working conditions that are important to you.

4. Complete the worksheets that will help you communicate your strengths as they relate to this company and job. You may want to use material you developed in chapter 3, "Preparing: Your Brain."

Interview Practice Worksheet 1—Strengths

List five areas of particular strength.

1. _____

2. _____

3. _____

4. _____

5. _____

Interview Practice Worksheet 2—Match Skills

List five ways your skills match the needs of the job.

1. _____

    _____

2. _____

    _____

3. _____

    _____

4. _____

    _____

5. _____

    _____

Interview Practice Worksheet 3—Information Goals

List four things of importance to you in any job you take.

1. _____

    _____

2. _____

    _____

3. _____

    _____

4. _____

    _____

Interview Practice Worksheet 4—Overcoming Weakness

Describe the major weakness in your background for this job and how you have corrected, or will correct, it.

Weakness: _____

_____

_____

Correction: _____

_____

_____

Interview Practice Worksheet 5—Personal Qualities

List below the personal qualities that you would like to communicate in the interview.

1. _____

_____

2. _____

_____

3. _____

_____

4. _____

_____

5. _____

_____

Section II: For the Employer

Your job in the practice interview is to act as the employer. Basically you are judging whether or not you want the candidate as a member of your team. The complete directions for doing this are provided in this section. You will, however, have to use your imagination in playing the role of the employer and your intelligence in making judgments about the candidate. The more realistic you can make this practice, the more helpful it will be to your partner.

1. Read the job description and the organizational description that were written for the exercise. Put yourself in the place of an employer in that company. Imagine you are the owner or the manager of a large department. You may fill in more details in your mind than you are given.

2. Read the resume of the candidate. See what experience and background the candidate is bringing to the job described.

3. Before you begin the interview, review the questions you will ask and the rating sheet at the end of this section. This will help you remember what to look for during the interview. It is best if you complete the rating sheet immediately after the interview. Be sure to read all the directions before beginning the interview.

4. When both you and the candidate have finished your preparation, sit at a table or desk with an empty chair next to it. The candidate should leave the room and reenter it. THIS BEGINS THE INTERVIEW.

5. Get up to greet the candidate as he or she enters. Hold out your hand to the candidate, introduce yourself, and ask the candidate to sit in the empty chair.

6. Ask the candidate the practice interview questions, one at a time, allowing plenty of time for the answer.

*Practice Interview
Questions*

1. Can you describe a typical day on your present job?

2. What do you consider your single most important idea or accomplishment on the job or in school?

3. What do you think it takes to be effective in the job for which you are applying?

4. What has been the greatest failure of your business or school life?

5. Why are you leaving your present job?

6. Describe the best boss you can imagine.

7. What was your major or best subject in school?

8. Tell me about your career goals.

9. Do you have any questions you would like to ask me?

10. Why do you think you are the best person for this job?

You may ask follow-up or additional questions if you wish.

Use the Interview Practice Rating Sheet to rate the candidate's performance. Then discuss the ratings with your partner. The purpose of the ratings is to help your partner figure out which interview skills need work.

Interview Practice Rating Sheet

Give the candidate a mark of 1, 2, 3, or 4 on each of the following items. 1 = poor; 2 = fair; 3 = good; 4 = excellent

__   1. Established eye contact

__   2. Addressed you by name correctly after you introduced yourself.

__   3. Smiled during the greeting.

__   4. Waited to sit until invited to do so.

__   5. Sat up straight, but in a natural position.

__   6. Did not fidget with nails, hair, clothes, etc.

__   7. Communicated interest and enthusiasm.

__   8. Mentioned her or his own strengths.

__   9. Showed how strengths were related to the job.

__   10. Did not contradict things on the resume.

__   11. Did not make bad jokes.

__   12. Answered the question about weakness in a straightforward way.

__   13. Said how the weakness was being worked on.

__   14. Did not appear nervous when talking about the weakness.

__   15. Reasons for leaving the present job showed motivation to do better.

__   16. The description of the best boss seemed like the kind of boss you would like to be.

__   17. Career goals were related to the job being applied for.

__   18. Mentioned courses in school related to the job being applied for.

__   19. Did not ask about salary or benefits.

__   20. Did not ask about hours of work.

__   21. Communicated energy.

__   22. Seemed like someone you could trust to carry out the work.

___ 23. Seemed to work well with others.

___ 24. Questions showed interest in the work to be performed.

___ 25. Overall rating.

Final score: Add the score on all the items.

A final word to the job seeker: The highest possible total score is 100. A score over 85 means you did very well overall. Whether your total score was high or low, look at the score on individual items. Remember 4 was the highest possible individual item score, and 1 was the lowest. Identify the areas in which further work is needed. Then review the appropriate chapters of this book to create a winning interview.

APPENDIX B: Bibliography of Related Readings

Books about Job Hunting

Bloch, Deborah P. *How to Get and Get Ahead on Your First Job.* Lincolnwood, Ill.: VGM Career Horizons, 1988.

Bloch, Deborah P. *How to Make the Right Career Moves.* Lincolnwood, Ill.: VGM Career Horizons, 1990.

Bloch, Deborah P. *How to Write a Winning Resume.* rev. ed. Lincolnwood, Ill.: VGM Career Horizons, 1990.

Bolles, Richard N. *What Color Is Your Parachute?* Berkeley: Ten Speed Press, 1991.

Books about Building Your Confidence

Covey, S. R. *The Seven Habits of Highly Effective People.* New York: Simon and Schuster, 1989.

Dardik, I. and D. Waitley. *Quantum Fitness.* New York: Simon and Schuster, 1984.

Gawain, S. *Creative Visualization.* New York: Bantam Books, 1979.

Goleman, D. *The Meditative Mind.* rev. ed. Los Angeles: J. P. Tarcher, 1988.

***Books about
Interviewing Written for
Employers***

Dobrish, C., R. Wolff, and B. Zevnick. *Hiring the Right Person for the Right Job.* New York: Franklin Watts, 1984.

Drake, J. *The Effective Interviewer: A Guide for Managers.* New York: AMACOM, 1989.

Eder, R.W. and G.R. Ferris, eds. *The Employment Interview: Theory, Research and Practice.* Troy, N.Y.: Sage, 1989.

Gratus, J. *Successful Interviewing: How to Find and Keep the Best People.* New York: Penguin, 1988.

Wendover, R.W. *Smart Hiring: The Complete Guide for Recruiting Employees.* Engelwood, Colo.: MSP Inc., 1989.